JAMES BONNEY M.P.

by Ian Buckley

Published by Playdead Press 2017

© Ian Buckley 2017

Ian Buckley has asserted his rights under the Copyright, Design and Patents Act, 1988, to be identified as the authors of this work.

A CIP catalogue record for this book is available from the British Library.

ISBN 978-1-910067-48-2

Caution
All rights whatsoever in this play are strictly reserved and application for performance should be sought through the author before rehearsals begin. No performance may be given unless a license has been obtained.

This book is sold subject to the condition that it shall not by way of trade or otherwise, be lent, resold, hired out, or otherwise circulated without the publisher's prior consent in any form of binding or cover other than that in which it is published and without a similar condition including this condition being imposed on the subsequent purchaser.

Playdead Press
www.playdeadpress.com

James Bonney MP was first produced at The White Bear Theatre, London, June 20 – July 8 2017, with the following cast:

James Bonney	Andrew Loudon
Christine Bonney	Karen McCaffrey
Kate Bonney	Elian West
Jennifer Allen	Louise Tyler
Malcolm Rose	Ciaran Lonsdale
George Jenner	Malcolm Jeffries

Directed by Georgia Leanne Harris
Designed by Oscar Selfridge
Lighting and stage management by White Bear Theatre Associates
Produced by Ian Buckley
Casting Director Andrew Davies
Publicity Kevin Wilson

Ian Buckley

Ian went to Christ's College Cambridge from the Elliott Comprehensive, Putney. He gained an Honours degree in English Literature from Christ's College plus a soccer blue for good measure. He continued his studies at the University of Kent where he gained an MA researching the works of Sean O'Casey.

Having spent most of his school/university years analysing and assessing the works of other playwrights, Ian decided it was time to become a playwright himself. It's what he's been doing ever since.

Ian has had a number of plays performed on the London fringe: *The Tailors' Last Stand* (Baron's Court Theatre 2013); *Keeping Faith* (The King's Head); *Picassos' Artful Occupation* (Barons Court 2014); *The Moment We Met* (Barons Court 2015); *Realife TV* (Barons Court 2016); *First Timers* (The Duke's Head); *Suits and Blouses* (The Room at The Orange Tree); *Down The River* (Theatre Royal, Stratford East, touring show); *Tainted Love* (The Young Actors' Theatre).

He's been shortlisted for the following playwriting competitions: the Verity Bargate Award; the Maddermarket Award; The Bruntwood Manchester Royal Exchange (long shortlisted with *The Return*); the Brockley Jack 'Write Now Three' competition.

He's had a play on BBC Radio Four, *Changing Gear*, re-broadcast in translation on Hessische Rundfunk in Germany, who also broadcast *The Revolutionary*.

He was granted an Arts Council Writer's Bursary to complete his play *Dr Richter and Pero* - about the first ever meeting of Lenin and Trotsky which took place in London in 1902.

The rumour that he's made any money from his pen is entirely unfounded.

HOW THE PLAY CAME ABOUT

The Labour Party has always been a strange beast to me, situated as I am to the left of it.

If in the UK we have one political party that represents the interests and aims of capitalism (the Conservative & Unionist Party), why isn't there another party that represents the interests and aims of its alternative - socialism?

Instead we have the Labour Party.

Too often it is dominated by right-wing social democrats who are more than happy with the status quo. James Bonney, my play's 'hero' is one such. A 'moderate', a moderniser, a New Labourite. A man who bridles at the word socialism. A man whose natural home is really the Conservative Party.

He represents the shadow cabinet ministers who resigned en masse to get rid of Corbyn in June 2016. He represents the Blairites who brief against Jeremy Corbyn as easily as breathing. He represents the 'false choice' the Labour Party has for too long offered the people of this country.

And then there is Corbyn - from the left of the Labour Party. Recently twice elected on a huge members' mandate as party leader, he inclines more to the policies of the post-war Attlee government than to the Thatcherite policies of the Blair-Brown-Mandelson years.

And the two sides slug it out. It's a no-holds barred, vicious, sometimes dirty battle. It draws in and uses family. It makes or breaks friendships. It's a battle for control of the Labour Party.

That's what my comedy is about - this battle. As a socialist I know which side I hope emerges victorious. As a playwright I willingly give both sides equal weight.

CHARACTERS

James Bonney   M.P. Islington Central (Labour)

Christine Bonney   His wife. A teacher

Kate Bonney   His daughter, a post-graduate student working on a PhD (NGO's)

Malcolm Rose   Challenger for Islington nomination. Labour Party

Jennifer Allen   Bonney's Secretary

George Jenner   Party Agent, Bonney's constituency – Labour Party

TIME: the present

SYNOPSIS: the life and loves of a sitting Labour MP as he comes under attack from a young militant who has designs on both his seat and his daughter

PROLOGUE

Hubbub of voices.

Enter George Jenner and James Bonney

JENNER: Ladies and gentlemen. Brothers and sisters. Your loyal and hard-working Member of Parliament, James Bonney!

Clapping and cheering. Bonney calls for silence

BONNEY: It's a lovely day! And a lovely event! A family affair. A chance to relax. To be human. Because that's what it's all about. That's what our Party was founded for – to help people. Ordinary people, working people. To help them to a better life.

And no matter what happens out there; (*Gesture to outside world*) no matter how many set-backs I receive out there, an event like this restores me! Re-charges my batteries! Sends me out a new man! We're a family, and we're part of a larger family, the one we call humankind! Like all families we have our ups and downs, our arguments. (*Polite laughter*) A family without dissent is a tyranny! We welcome argument, dispute, the battle of ideas! Because at the end of the day we know they are just that. Arguments within the family. And we know that in the end, when the differences have been aired, we will all join hands as brothers and sisters and work for each other! Work to realise the great ideals this Party was founded upon. And I want to be part of that work. I want to be lifted and inspired by that struggle for a better world.

So. Eat your fill. Drink as much as you ought. And here's to us. To people! Our kind of people!

He raises his glass and drinks to great applause.

BLACKOUT

SCENE ONE

Bonney's house. Christine, with rubber gloves, is scraping at a door with a black and decker hot-air, paint-stripping tool.

Ring on bell.

Exit Christine. Re-enter with Jenner.

JENNER: He said seven.

CHRISTINE: He never...

JENNER: I've written it down...

He takes out a diary opens it.

CHRISTINE: ...mentioned it to me. But then he never does.

JENNER: You look busy.

CHRISTINE: You look thin. What you been up to?

JENNER: Directing.

CHRISTINE: What?

JENNER: The campaign. For James.

Christine continues with work

CHRISTINE: James, James. He's back to his habits. If he tries hard he could have another coronary by Christmas and although I do find him irritating at times I'd rather he were alive on the whole. (*She points to a plastic bucket stage right*) Would you?

Jenner fetches it

JENNER: I'm sorry I've not been round...

CHRISTINE: I've missed you terribly.

JENNER: Really?

CHRISTINE: But of course. Look what I've filled my lonely nights up with.

JENNER: I shouldn't say this. Treacherous really, James a friend, and work-mate and um... well kick me out if you like. I mean I'd piss off and feel I deserved it, and that's a promise. But erm... well... well I s'ppose it's obvious that I feel very... feel very...

CHRISTINE: (*Inspecting the door*) Fancy-work's the worst.

JENNER: God, this is hard, but well, what I want to say is... I love you.

CHRISTINE: Could you lay another paper?

Jenner takes a newspaper from a pile nearby and puts one under an exposed corner of the door.

JENNER: That's why I've not been round.

CHRISTINE: (*Lifting table*) Right under.

Jenner pushes it further under

JENNER: To put you out of my mind. And I succeeded. Until tonight. Tonight the dams burst.

CHRISTINE: (*Surveying stripped door*) That's very clean.

JENNER: But I've told you now and I only wish I knew how you felt about me.

CHRISTINE: Does that pass the test?

JENNER: Um?

CHRISTINE: Is it clean?

JENNER: Yes.

CHRISTINE: You're not just saying?

JENNER: No it's really... clean.

CHRISTINE: Apart from the burns. See! (*She shows Jenner*)

JENNER: Christine! Did you hear...?

CHRISTINE: Just to be sure. Can you...? (*Jenner takes hold of door*) And gently pull. (*Jenner does. Leans past door towards her*)

JENNER: I bloody fancy you. (*Arm of his jacket smoulders*)

CHRISTINE: George dear, you're alight. (*Jenner jumps back. Looks at jacket an instant. Ignores it*) Didn't I tell you to watch out?

JENNER: Did you? (*Smacks jacket*)

CHRISTINE: No immolation in Waltmore Crescent thank you! (*She determinedly starts to strip door*) If I suddenly perspire, wipe my face with that sponge.

She indicates a sponge nearby. Jenner nods assent. Stands watching her, silent.

> And if you'd just roll my sleeve up you can relax while I strip.

Jenner rolls her sleeve up then walks to chair and slumps in it

> If only they made doors like this now.

JENNER: Look I'm sorry. Please forget what I said. Just testing. Just for a laugh.

CHRISTINE: I knew that silly. We must get James to cut down. The doctors have said he should but according to him they're all alarmists who want to turn him into a neurotic hypochondriac... I thought the new secretary might help, but she lets him do as he likes. (*Pause*) Are you listening?

JENNER: Yes. Yes.

CHRISTINE: Suggestions?

JENNER: No.

Sound of front door opening

CHRISTINE: I do not believe it.

Enter James Bonney. Slings briefcase onto floor, flops onto sofa, undoes tie

BONNEY: George you punctual bastard. I thought I'd beat you. I'm early mate, early! And how's my wife - stripping us back to basics?

CHRISTINE: You're drunk.

BONNEY: Half a bloody mary and a weak bitter. (*Sniffs*) Can I smell burning?

JENNER: (*Holding up sleeve*) I got in the way.

BONNEY: What were you up to? (*Jenner colours*) She's deadly with that. Carbonise your balls in a blink. Ahem... campaign strategy wasn't it? Fire away. I'm all ears.

JENNER: The approach has been support for their hard-working member. Emphasis on righting a wrong. You're seen as a trusting servant of the community despicably stabbed in the back by sinister ideologues, is making inroads into the stay-at-home section of the party. In a word, we're winning.

BONNEY: Excellent. And you do it all for love. The sort of loyalty I inspire sometimes amazes even me George.

JENNER: I've arranged a meeting.

BONNEY: What a Trojan.

JENNER: Thursday.

BONNEY: Can't make Thursday. I'm sorry James but Thursday is one day I cannot do.

JENNER: But that was agreed.

BONNEY: Change of plan. Pressure of events. All that bollocks.

JENNER: When can you make?

BONNEY: Not next week at all.

JENNER: But we don't have much time.

BONNEY: Full diary next week.

JENNER: You can't let them down.

BONNEY: Semi-national commitments mate... affairs of almost-national importance. (*Bonney sits down. Feet out. Relaxes*) Doing a grand job,

George. (*Fit of coughing from James*) My man on the ground. My eyes and ears. Keep it up.

Picks up TV guide. Flicks through

JENNER: This is the second time. They won't like it.

BONNEY: Then they can lump it, no I don't mean that. The week after... Tuesday. I'll be there. Don't get frayed nerves. There's no problem.

JENNER: It's better to build your base...

BONNEY: ...Than not to. That's why I place my trust in George Jenner, best fixer in the business...

JENNER: But if I can't even arrange a meeting with people who want to support you.

BONNEY: What sort of an agent are you? A good one, and you'll arrange it the week after and I'll be there. I promise. Football on the box. (*Indicates & moves to TV*) We'll talk over that.

JENNER: I'll phone tomorrow. (*He begins to exit*)

BONNEY: You're not going?

JENNER: If you can't take this seriously...

BONNEY: But I am. Sit down. Have a drink.

JENNER: Tomorrow.

Jenner exits. Christine continues to work on door. Bonney puts his arms around her waist from behind.

BONNEY: George was a bit...

CHRISTINE: Off.

BONNEY: Exactly. He worries me. He can't relax. And unpredictable. Fancy storming out like that, like a little child.

CHRISTINE: Off, I said! (*He doesn't move*) If you don't I'll cremate you. (*Bonney jumps back with alacrity*)

BONNEY: Who's in a mood?

CHRISTINE: Not me.

BONNEY: You are.

CHRISTINE: I'm not.

BONNEY: Are.

CHRISTINE: Not.

BONNEY: I can tell.

CHRISTINE: Will you go away?

BONNEY: Now is that any way to speak to your husband. Who thinks so much of you he's taking you out for a meal... an Anniversary meal. Yes, I've not forgotten.

Christine looks at James. He looks back and smiles. She melts a little, blower in hand

CHRISTINE: James... really?

Bonney approaches. Pushes blower out of way as its pointing at him

BONNEY: Being nasty for nothing and all the time I've been making arrangements.

CHRISTINE: Oh dear. (*Suddenly tearful*) I feel awful. (*They hug*) It's just, I haven't seen you for so long. I can't help myself in the end.

BONNEY: 'S alright. (*They kiss*) Can't be good tempered all the time. I mean I'm very even-tempered but even I have my days.

CHRISTINE: Where?

BONNEY: Um?

CHRISTINE: The meal?

BONNEY: Oh, the meal. Secret.

CHRISTINE: Ooh, I love surprises. When?

BONNEY: This week or the week after. It's um... entirely up to you.

CHRISTINE: (*Scowl of suspicion*) James. If you're making this up...

BONNEY: Chris! How could you? I couldn't arrange an exact date till I'd consulted you. Now, when are you free?

CHRISTINE: Monday... or Thursday.

BONNEY: O.K. let me see... (*He takes a diary out of his pocket*) ...No ...No ...well, we'll leave it till next week. No hurry.

He stands up. Walks to middle of room

CHRISTINE: James, you bloomin' well...

BONNEY: Sssssssh. Quiet. I must have quiet. (*He stands still. Let's trunk drop forward. Breathes*

>   *deeply. Then gradually draws himself back up to his full height. Eyes closed*) Intrigues dissolve. Alliances disappear. And away. And away.

He stands quite still. Christine looks on sceptically

BONNEY: I'm into a trance quicker than a Shaman these days. Mastering my mood. Countering strain. (*Christine finishes with door. takes off rubber gloves*) Be nice to Jamesy.

CHRISTINE: Give me one good reason.

BONNEY: Knackered. Knocked up. Need warmth and sun, not the old cold shoulder.

CHRISTINE: You're never around for any sort of shoulder.

BONNEY: So it's precious to me when I am. I'm so eternally busy. I will try to get home more. I promise. Now, sit down, feet up. Tonight let me look after you.

BLACKOUT

END OF SCENE

SCENE TWO

Spotlight different area of stage

Jennifer and Bonney embracing passionately. Bonney tears himself away. Pause. Panting subsides

JENNIFER: Feel free.

BONNEY: Sorry... I'm not in the mood.

JENNIFER: It's impolite to say.

BONNEY: At least I'm honest.

JENNIFER: A mixed blessing.

BONNEY: And what good would I be? You must've felt... I wasn't heart and soul.

JENNIFER: It's not your soul I'm after.

BONNEY: You don't understand. I feel guilty.

JENNIFER: Pull the other one.

BONNEY: I do. I love my wife. Not in the same way as I love... but a deep way, a complex way – companionship, caring, loyalty, respect. And conscience is nagging, Jen'. Nag, nag, nag. I'm not a hardened liar, and I'm having to lie, lie upon lie, and the more I tell the more I have to tell. And I'm not used to it. I mean, I've never done this before. You are the first, the absolute first. I mean I have resisted temptation for twenty years. For two decades I've marched purely through life – morals up, conscience-clean. And not for want of opportunity I can tell you. There's

	women've fancied me, and made it obvious too, but I wouldn't wear it, Jen'. I've cured their lust with a single look.
JENNIFER:	We've each of us only one life. Why do I devote mine to a married man who says he's in love with his wife while snatching full-on kisses with me whenever he can? Have you thought of that?
BONNEY:	Yes.
JENNIFER:	I don't moan. I have a fatal attraction for chocolate fudge and older men, but I've learned to live with it. Can't you do the same?
BONNEY:	You can't liken a wife to chocolate fudge.
JENNIFER:	(*Picks up diary. Opens it*) Tonight the Chamber of Commerce. Tomorrow, Unite regional council. Friday Lord Mayor's reception...
BONNEY:	What can I do?
JENNIFER:	Leave her. Or leave me. Select Committee, Integration and Advancement following Monday...
BONNEY:	Jen', will you pay attention?
JENNIFER:	(*Puts down diary*) Entirely captive audience. Sir.
BONNEY:	(*Deep breath*) Our relationship's got to change. I propose the following. As before in every way, bar one. No touching. A strong

partnership where all that's cut out. No temptation offered on either side.

Jennifer who has sat down on a hard chair, pulls her skirt down and sits up straight

The past is rubbed out. Well?

JENNIFER: Fine. Tonight you've got a clash between...

BONNEY: Have you been listening?

JENNIFER: ...A clash between a one-day conference on security in the workplace or a meeting with your local Party to discuss your voting record.

BONNEY: Buggar the last. Bloody Rose and his henchmen calling me to account. I'll go to the first.

Jennifer writes in diary

JENNIFER: (*Marks it in*) Now, if you're ready... I'll drive you to the House.

Exit Jennifer. Bonney combs hair in mirror

BONNEY: (*To himself*) Done it. Told her. Can't mess about at my age. I'm too old. (*He takes small cream container. Puts oil on face*) Dry skin. Look't it. Wrinkles. Time flies faster and bloody faster. I've still not got anywhere. When the hell will I? I've got a brain on my shoulders. I'm not stupid. What's holding me back?

He walks out of spotlight, across stage to party offices area. He shouts

James. James! (*Enter Jenner with local constituency maps in area, in hand. Smoking*)

Am I capable, or am I not?

JENNER: Of what?

BONNEY: At my job.

JENNER: Is this a trick question?

BONNEY: Deadly serious.

JENNER: One hundred per cent capable.

BONNEY: Of sticking my foot in it?

JENNER: Have you seen the balance of forces?

BONNEY: Why can't I be a whizz-kid? Shooting through ministries, making a stir, getting things done?

JENNER: The pro and anti Jameses?

BONNEY: I'll tell you why. I'm not hungry enough. I expect my works to speak for themselves. I could do with a bit more bobbing and scraping. None of this voting with your conscience bollocks.

JENNER: It's a terrible thing conscience bollocks.

BONNEY: It's a disease.

JENNER: We may die unknown but we'll die proud.

BONNEY: I've not succumbed to the blandishments of power.

JENNER: You've not had the chance. (*They study the map*)

BONNEY: Chicken and egg. I've not had the chance because I've not succumbed.

JENNER: Can I bring us back to earth? Rose is gaining votes. I've done a mates' check through the branches. He's on the up. It'd help if you put in the odd appearance. Letting us down for the management meeting was fucking disastrous. Especially since I'd changed the date before. Twice.

BONNEY: George please. Life's simpler for you. You're single. And politically you work on one level. I work on two.

JENNER: My level's more important. Lose it, you lose everything.

BONNEY: What's all this about losing? We're not losing anything are we?

JENNER: Why can't you make the meeting next week?

BONNEY: Not at liberty to say but I may, stress may, be in line for a job, no you didn't hear me say that George - keep it under your hat 'cos it's all hush-hush but it has something to do with my absences right now. Yes?

JENNER: That's all very well but...

BONNEY: No buts. We have to work as a team. You have to work harder here to make up for my inability so to do. But I will get down to a management meeting soon. Promise.

FADE OUT

END OF SCENE

SCENE THREE

Party offices. Rose is watching leaflets print off on printer. Kate stacks leaflets

KATE: How many?

ROSE: Three.

KATE: Three what?

ROSE: Thousand.

KATE: Two thousand eight hundred too many. People don't read them. They screw them up and chuck them.

Rose takes leaflets out of tray, and jiggles with them to get them squared, hands them to Kate

ROSE: Not ours. Ours are special. We speak in ordinary language…

KATE: To ordinary people.

ROSE: Precisely.

They continue folding leaflets

KATE: Will you try to oust my Dad?

They both fold leaflets in silence. Rose folds them faster than Kate. Kate increases her pace to catch up with him. She catches up and folds faster

ROSE: Race eh?

KATE: Sixteen. Seventeen.

ROSE: Two thousand and five. Two thousand and six.

KATE: Why?

ROSE: What?

KATE: Attack my father.

ROSE: A man has to do…

KATE: Be serious.

ROSE: I support different policies. It's perfectly straightforward and legal and healthy. It's called democracy. The battle of ideas. Rules are laid down, opposing sides take the field, and play to win. When the majority accept your ideas you've won. Why your old man has to make such a song and dance about it I don't know.

KATE: You can hardly expect a slap on the back when you've called for a vote of no-confidence in him.

ROSE: If he'd adopt a few of our policies I'd call off the vote.

KATE: But he doesn't think they're right. (*Pause. They fold leaflets*)

ROSE: Well I do.

KATE: He works hard.

ROSE: To work hard for the wrong policies is no recommendation.

KATE: They're only wrong in your eyes.

ROSE: You say it as if it's an illness.

KATE: Just... why can't you live and let live?

ROSE: Kate, you are so naive. Excuse me for saying it but you are.

KATE: And you have the wisdom of Solomon?

ROSE: Not quite. But I'll teach you what I know if you'll listen. And the first lesson is – you sometimes support someone you dislike against someone you like, because the former has what in your view are the right policies, and the latter doesn't. Now, as a person I like your old man... well I certainly don't dislike him. But as an M.P. he's a disaster.

KATE: He's got a lot of support round here.

ROSE: He's addicted to privatising everything. Madly in love with the idea no human activity in our brief and messy lives should occur without a healthy profit being made out of it. In fact why isn't he in the Tory Party? That's his home. They may be a shade keener on seeing foxes torn apart and the bloody bits smeared over their Eton-bound progeny's bewildered faces but these are details. On the essentials they're one – cheer-leaders for UK Holdings. Evangelists for the country as company, the 'let's-be-the-highest-rated-island-to-float-on-the-stock-exchange' brigade. It's not what we need. It's not why I joined the Party. James is a Tory Trojan-horse, a fifth-columnist undermining

	us from within. That's why I oppose him. It's not personal.
KATE:	I hate politics. All it does is divide.
ROSE:	Not true. It multiplies...
KATE:	Your enemies?
ROSE:	...Friends. It's the key to social progress.
KATE:	And may earn you a well-paid job where you'll be the centre of attention and think you're god's gift to the nation.
ROSE:	You're full of regressive ideas. I'll have to take your education in hand. It's a priority. Lesson one – a true activist always folds a leaflet neatly down the middle. Like so. (*Kate throws her pile of leaflets on the floor*) And isn't given to tantrums which can harm the march of progress.
KATE:	You are such a pain sometimes.
ROSE:	But you like me?
KATE:	No wonder you rub people up the wrong way.
ROSE:	People? Your father? The old guard? Who think they own the Party and wet-behind-the-ears upstarts like me should hang on 'til we're at least forty before we sit on closed committees and fart at the public like they do.
KATE:	You're completely arrogant.

ROSE: I speak my mind.

KATE: Lose your temper too easily.

ROSE: I feel guilty after.

KATE: Isn't it better to be nice to people than to feel bad about upsetting them.

ROSE: Who's perfect Kate? (*Rose takes a few piles of leaflets. Stuffs them into a carrier bag*) I'll pop round tonight. Stay if you're lucky.

KATE: How will I struggle through an afternoon without you? Every minute will seem like a month till then.

ROSE: (*Tongue in cheek*) And another thing – sarcasm is a manifestation of a person's inability to cope with life and should be ruthlessly excluded by progressive people such as ourselves.

KATE: (*Smiling*) So sorry comrade.

FADE DOWN

END OF SCENE

SCENE FOUR

Jennifer's flat in London. Fairly pleasant bed-sit. Large window. Usual bed-sit furniture.

Enter Jennifer, followed by Bonney who has bottle of wine in his hand. Bonney puts wine on table and flops into sofa, loosens tie, undoes shirt.

BONNEY: ...That bloody debate. How long did I have to wait? (*Expression of disgust. Jennifer opens the wine while Bonney's speaking. She fills a glass and hands to Bonney*) Integrating communities? I'm good at that. I know how to create harmony between different ethnic groups with contrasting outlooks on life. (*Takes a good drink. savours it*)

Time I was able to get in the debate, it'd all gone flat. (*Another good gulp*) Mmmm. Nice wine. (*Resumes*) 'We can't let things drift. Have to take action. Give the law teeth...' (*Another swig*) I've got experience in my own bloody constituency for god sake.

JENNIFER: Can you relax...?

BONNEY: Later.

JENNIFER: No now. I'll help.

Bonney stands up, sheepishly Jennifer stands opposite him. Jennifer flops from trunk. Bonney follows suit. They slowly rise

BONNEY: I indicated I wanted to speak...

JENNIFER: Ssssssh... (*She swings from right to left. Bonney follows suit. Silence*)

BONNEY: Just because I'm not a big gob.

JENNIFER: Clear you mind. (*Bonney stops following Jennifer's exercises*)

BONNEY: I can't.

JENNIFER: You've hardly tried.

BONNEY: Hundreds of times. Heavy breathing. Body flops. All that.

JENNIFER: You've no self-control.

BONNEY: Not with yoga.

JENNIFER: Not with most things.

BONNEY: Uh?

JENNIFER: You get too worked up.

BONNEY: My bloody job'd work up an angel

JENNIFER: And you're no angel.

BONNEY: I've got qualities a bit like an angel.

Jennifer clears a space in the middle of the room

JENNIFER: Lie down. (*Bonney looks startled*) On your stomach.

BONNEY: Remember what we said...

JENNIFER: Oh really. I hereby promise not to commit any obscene act upon the body of the man. (*Bonney who has taken his jacket off, lies down as requested*) You're lying on the beach. Hot sun. Clean sand. You feel good. You unwind. (*She kneels down by his side, gently massages*

31

his shoulders) Here... (*Then down a little*) ...and here. (*She massages but stays in the 'safe' areas of the back*) You feel heavy. (*She massages the back of his neck*) Your limbs are heavy. You feel calm. Peaceful. You rel-a-a-ax... reel... ax...

She quietly stands up, tiptoes to chair sits. Triumph. Bonney suddenly jerks his head up and looks at her

BONNEY: Can I get up? (*He stands up*)

JENNIFER: You're supposed to be relaxing.

BONNEY: (*Walking to sofa*) ...Pillock ignores me on purpose.

JENNIFER: Which pillock?

BONNEY: The speaker-pillock. I'm never in a debate when it matters. I'm either trying to get in, or... (*Jennifer walks to her portable radio. she turns it up loud. we see Bonney's mouth moving but we can't hear what he's saying. he stops talking. she turns the radio down*) That, I take it, is called making your point?

JENNIFER: Why don't you try and get some sleep? Curl up on the sofa. I'll call you when it's time.

BONNEY: I'm too excited. I need to go for a run or... pass the wine.

JENNIFER: No.

BONNEY: Whaddyou mean no?

JENNIFER: You've had enough. You'll misbehave.

BONNEY: Rubbish! Give me the wine. (*Jennifer doesn't*) I'm warning you. If you don't give it, I'll take it. (*She holds bottle firmly, and stays where she is*) Right. We'll see about that.

Bonney stands. Rubs hands. Begins to 'stalk' Jennifer. As Bonney approaches Jennifer backs away, holding bottle all the while. She gets some furniture – a chair, or table between her and Bonney. He lunges for bottle. She snatches it away. He moves to right, she to left. He finally makes a dive round table but she's too quick for him. He chases and dives at her, misses her and falls on floor. She laughs. He picks himself up, starts to go for her again. The walk speeds to a run. Finally James catches her from behind, holds her tight. They fall on sofa, spilling wine. He takes bottle from her, swigs back few mouthfuls, then they go quiet. Bonney kisses her. She's quite willing.

BONNEY: This is ridiculous.

JENNIFER: I know.

BONNEY: What the hell am I doing?

JENNIFER: Making a fool of yourself. (*Kisses her again*)

BONNEY: You're young enough to be my daughter.

JENNIFER: Not quite.

BONNEY: You don't want to…?

JENNIFER: Be better if we didn't.

While they say these lines, and those that follow they start to take off their clothes.

BONNEY: After what we promised.

JENNIFER: A pledge. An undertaking. (*More clothes off*)

BONNEY: To avoid the physical.

JENNIFER: The purely sexual.

BONNEY: To forget about touching.

JENNIFER: To stop that side.

BONNEY: So we've got to be strong. It'll do us good.

JENNIFER: A lot of good.

BONNEY: Will-power! Have a bit of it. (*As they embrace*)

JENNIFER: I do.

BONNEY: Then have more.

JENNIFER: I can't.

BONNEY: Then it's not enough.

JENNIFER: And what about you? You show the way.

BONNEY: I do. The wrong way.

JENNIFER: You've always shown me that way. When I first met you I could feel it. I walked into your office in reply to the advert and my knees were knocking. You were so charming. So in charge. I sat down on the chair you showed me and you took the situation and me over. And you kept looking at me with a look that was half polite, and half something else not so easy to describe. I said, Jennifer leave right now, don't take the job, even if he offers because you'll be going the wrong way. But I didn't leave then, and I can't stop now. You seduced me. Took advantage of a poor employee, abused your position, used your experience to turn my head. And I loved it, because I played my part too. So don't ask me to exercise will-power. I don't want to, I'm not going to. One day I want to live with you, openly. Get married, who knows? It's you who has to make up your mind.

FADE DOWN

END OF SCENE

SCENE FIVE

Party offices. Table. Chairs.

Enter Bonney and Jenner.

BONNEY: Have you organised the troops?

JENNER: I have.

BONNEY: And are we home and dry?

JENNER: By my calculations... just.

BONNEY: What's 'just' supposed to mean? We should be ahead by a mile.

JENNER: Rose works hard. He's tactically sharp. He's sincere too. From the heart.

BONNEY: My God, my God... you joined the fan-club?

JENNER: My observations.

BONNEY: So I don't speak from the heart?

JENNER: Locally you've not been seen to speak from any part of the anatomy for years.

BONNEY: Parliamentary tasks. No wonder Rose can spend more time than me drumming up support. What else has he sodding well got to do?

JENNER: If it wasn't that some think he's a bit too ambitious we'd have our backs well and truly to the wall.

BONNEY: Don't exaggerate...

JENNER: You asked me.

BONNEY: Did you do the... um... other thing?

JENNER: He's clean.

BONNEY: Did you really search?

JENNER: I'm employed as your agent not a snooper.

BONNEY: So you didn't. Let me down again George.

JENNER: Stop finding excuses! You have to keep working. Descend from the dizzy heights of S.W.1. and get among the locals. Shore up your base here. Their hard work put you into parliament – show a smidgeon of gratitude.

BONNEY: George please. You talk as if he's won. If you've done your job...

JENNER: I've done my best...

BONNEY: Then we're laughing. (*Pause*)

JENNER: There is one irritating matter keeps cropping up.

BONNEY: Um?

JENNER: They're spreading rumours.

BONNEY: About what?

JENNER: You. A whiff of scandal.

BONNEY: Scandal? Me?

JENNER: Hardly worth repeating, but they say you're... well... having it off with your secretary.

BONNEY: You're joking?

JENNER: Do I look like I am?

BONNEY: Come on you're...? I don't... (*Jenner indicates he's serious*) What a diabolical bloody lie!

JENNER: Members listen – truth... lies...

BONNEY: Why didn't I know about this?

JENNER: I had to make sure it was... general.

BONNEY: Who d'you mean 'they'?

JENNER: Your opponents...?

BONNEY: Which ones? I've got thousands of sodding Opponents. You mean Rose? You mean everyone on the left? Ten people? Twenty?

JENNER: I mean a hard core of them. A few.

BONNEY: What's a few for Christ's sake?

JENNER: Between one and a hundred? I don't have a number. And not just on the left. It's affected your work in the constituency they say. You miss your surgery regularly. The number of meetings you haven't made goes up and up...

BONNEY: Don't keep on about meetings. I want names. I want a full and detailed list of all the...

JENNER: I'd name half the local Party. (*Bonney, deep breathing exercises*)

Bonney mimes lifting someone off the floor by their coat lapels, and then shaking them back and forwards

BONNEY: Aaaaaaaaaaaaaarrrrrrgh! Don't leave me in the same room! There will be murder committed, so help me, there will be murder.

Telephone rings. Jenner answers.

Bonney has gone into a sort of trance, holding his chest with palm of right hand.

JENNER: (*Holding out telephone to Bonney*) The Guardian. (*Bonney marches to telephone, still holding chest*)

BONNEY: Speaking. (*He listens. begins to quote*) It is not a contest between Malcolm Rose and myself. It's a fight for an ideal. Democracy for the Party we love — the ordinary members having their say. Or the bigots of the politically correct school crushing us under their envy-filled jackboots.

(*Jenner grimaces. Bonney grins, does thumbs up to him*) I might have more for you tonight when I've had my meeting with the local party. (*Bonney puts phone down*)

JENNER: Was that wise?

BONNEY: I can fling shit too. Lousy, spineless, lick-spittles. Betray me? Slander me? Drag my name in the dirt? Right, that's it! That, my friend, is it. If any of them has done anything the tiniest, weeniest, fraction scandalous I shall dig it up and hang it out where no one, not even the most myopic of Party members

	can miss it. I shall stir up shite till the pong's so bad we all have to wear nose-clips.
JENNER:	(*After a pause*) Be careful what you say.
BONNEY:	Oh I will. Only the juiciest details. Only the most saucy will see light of day.
JENNER:	James this war with Rose is damaging enough in private. You use the columns of the Press for personal insults, we could end up losing the seat. The public don't like it. They'll vote with their feet.
BONNEY:	And what about the other side?
JENNER:	They've kept their comments private for the most part.
BONNEY:	D'you think they won't go public when it suits them?
JENNER:	They wouldn't dare unless they knew the rumour was true. Even then it's unlikely.
BONNEY:	Alright, alright. But if I see one word concerning my private life in print, or if so much as one person outside of our Party hears that rumour, I'll start on them. And I won't finish till I've wrecked the lot of them!

Pause. Bonney gathers breath

JENNER: It's not true... is it? (*Bonney looks at Jenner*) ...S'ppose it's the fact you're always together... arm in arm. You know people... always drawing conclusions.

BONNEY: Wrong ones. Jennifer and I are a close professional team.

JENNER: Of course.

BONNEY: I just won't go near Jennifer if that's how people are going to carry on. I'll write notes – "Sorry, can't talk, might be open to interpretation. Leave your reply on reverse. Till the next note. James".

Bonney does a trunk flop. Sways from side to side. Hurts his side enter Malcolm Rose. He moves to a chair on other side of room to Jenner and Bonney.

ROSE: Evening.

JENNER: 'Ning.

Bonney raises himself to full height.

Lets out a deep breath. Sits down.

Uncomfortable silence. Bonney grimaces in pain every now and again, but fights it back and it passes off.

BONNEY: You. (*Rose ignores him*) Do you feel proud? (*Bonney stands and moves nearer to rose who goes on ignoring him*) Swimming in muck. Or is it wading in crap?

ROSE: Are you addressing the scatology at me?

BONNEY: Who else in this room has a dirty mind?

ROSE: Apart from or including you?

BONNEY: I never mention a person's private affairs.

ROSE: What's held you back? You go for just about everything else.

BONNEY: Your private life's private. I've got standards.

ROSE: We can lie about each other to our back teeth so long as its political can we?

BONNEY: (*Shouting*) People's personal lives are nothing to do with politics. (*Stabbing his finger at Rose*) They're not included. They're separate. Out of bounds to anyone but themselves.

ROSE: (*Standing, toe to toe with Bonney*) I've got no interest whatsoever in your personal life, grubby or otherwise. You can shag a hole in the wall and I wouldn't blink I'm that liberal. I'm not your moral keeper. It's your politics that concern me.

Jenner walks across to Bonney. He puts himself between Bonney and Rose.

BONNEY: What d'you mean grubby? (*Jenner leads him away from Rose*) What's grubby about my personal life?

JENNER: James. Have a seat.

BONNEY: I want to know what he means by 'grubby'! He used the word, let him explain it.

JENNER: He didn't say it was grubby.

ROSE: 'Or otherwise', I said. It means I don't know if it is and I don't care either.

BONNEY: But you're spreading the poison. About... well about... (*Rose emphatically nods head in disagreement*) Does my daughter know?

ROSE: About what?

BONNEY: This rumour? This slander. This fabrication concerning – is it my secretary George? – yes my secretary and me.

ROSE: I've no idea. Why don't you ask her?

BONNEY: What d'you mean you've no idea? You live with her don't you?

ROSE: The subject's not been mentioned.

BONNEY: You're not involved in spreading it then?

ROSE: Correct.

BONNEY: You knew what I was talking about though.

ROSE: I imagined I'd guessed right.

BONNEY: Did you? Did you really? I'm not an idiot Malcolm.

ROSE: That's not the way I work. I wouldn't want to defeat you on that basis. It'd be a defeat for your private life, not your beliefs. As such, I'm not interested.

Bonney obviously thinking hard.

BONNEY: I don't believe you. I'm declaring war on you. (*James marches towards the exit, upstage right, turns, points finger aggressively at Rose*) I'll have you out of this Party before you do me. I'm not sitting down while you steamroller me into oblivion. It'll be my main political task for however long it takes. It'll work like a good boot up the backside for me whenever I start to slow down. To stop you and the rest of your holy 'we've-seen-the-light' left-wing crew taking over this constituency. I'll annihilate you. I'll destroy you!

Bonney turns on heel and walks off. Rose takes out 'new statesman', reads. Jenner approaches.

JENNER: Friends?

ROSE: Of sorts.

JENNER: Walk out of here now friend. Beat a tactical retreat. Bury the hatchet for the sake of Party unity.

ROSE: Sounds like committing hari kiri for the sake of party unity.

JENNER: Fight another seat. Where they want a contest.

ROSE: The fight's here. It's in every seat in the country with a right-wing prima donna undermining the fight for socialism.

JENNER: But why fight? Your policies are the same as his. It's only the speed of approach.

ROSE: His ground to a halt years ago.

JENNER: What would you need? Guarantees he might give?

ROSE: He wouldn't give them. And if he did I wouldn't trust them. No I feel confident. I'll take my chance with the vote... By the way, the 'rumour'... the scandal... I don't take much interest. It's a side-show as far as I'm concerned. Lots've people tell me they – I couldn't believe it – they heard it from you. 'Who told you', you ask. 'Jenner they say.' Are you sure you say? 'Yes. 'Mentioned it in passing'. I'm not saying that means much but well... 's a bit undiplomatic isn't it? A bit underhand? You being his agent? And friend? Seems a bit... well funny?

FADE DOWN

END OF SCENE

SCENE SIX

Same scene. An hour later. Rose and Bonney sit in silence Jenner enters.

BONNEY: (*Jumping to feet*) Well? Has sense prevailed?

JENNER: ...A temporary glitch.

BONNEY: Glitch? (*Rose makes victory sign with his hand*) What's that code for George? I lost?

JENNER: Of course not... They decided to refer it to a full members' vote. By fourteen to twelve.

BONNEY: But I'm the sitting MP. Backed by eighteen thousand last election. And fourteen are going to put my record to a vote of no-confidence?

ROSE: Fourteen gave you your chance in the first place.

BONNEY: (*To Rose*) You packed that committee. And you rigged that vote. I shall find out how. I shall go through all their credentials with a microscope. I shall call in National officers. I'll mount such a good campaign you'll be annihilated. This is my seat and you're not taking it away from me.

LIGHTS DOWN

END OF SCENE

SCENE SEVEN

Annual dance. Live dance band playing.

Bonney in men's toilets. Combing hair.

Inspecting face. Jenner peeing.

BONNEY: Well James?

JENNER: What?

BONNEY: Will they or won't they?

JENNER: Why should they?

BONNEY: Maximum effect. Sheer bitchiness. Say Christine just hears?

JENNER: But who from?

BONNEY: Don't ask me? These lies have a habit of surfacing when you least expect them.

JENNER: I can't see an advantage in telling her if you don't have to.

BONNEY: It may fade away. Most likely will. I've got to keep it in proportion. Ready? (*They exit from loo. Bonney walks up to Christine*) Shall we?

Bonney and Christine dance – a waltz.

They are good dancers – panache, timing, confidence, they have it all as they dance around stage, Bonney turns to smile at various people.

BONNEY: What a turn. What a step. Can we still?

CHRISTINE: We can, we can!

BONNEY: ...Move. Hold a woman – hold you – tight. Don't I love it? Haven't I always looked forward to it? (*Slight pause*) The swines! The ruthless bastards.

CHRISTINE: What on earth's the matter?

BONNEY: No. Why should we both suffer? To what end? Enjoy your dance.

CHRISTINE: James I want to know. If something's upset you.

BONNEY: Nothing. Nothing important. Why spread the poison?

CHRISTINE: I said I want to know.

BONNEY: How people in the same party... (*Nods head*)

CHRISTINE: Can what?

BONNEY: How they can stoop so low. The pits. (*Big smile at someone*) The bog of human existence.

Christine stops dancing.

CHRISTINE: James, will you tell me. (*Bonney whisks her away*)

BONNEY: You must keep dancing. They're here. Watching us.

Our every move. Waiting to swoop on the slightest sign of discord. (*Big smile all round. Music stops. They stop*)

CHRISTINE: My god, it must be bad.

BONNEY: Oh it is, it is. The slop-bucket of moral turpitude is cleanliness itself compared to this.

CHRISTINE: Then for god sake tell me what it is and put me out of my misery.

BONNEY: Someone – I don't know who but I have my suspicions – is spreading a rumour. The rumour is a vicious and particularly hurtful one, aimed below the belt, and it's got one intention and one intention only – to isolate, demoralise and discredit me.

CHRISTINE: Goodness.

BONNEY: There's worse to come. If it concerned just me I wouldn't give a toss. I'm armed against the rumour-mill. I've faced it all my political life. I'm immune. But others are caught up ...those nearest and dearest.

CHRISTINE: Who on earth do you mean?

BONNEY: You. Yes. Because the subject of this shitty rumour... (*Christine looks as if she's going to burst*) ...happens to be my relationship with...

CHRISTINE: Me?

BONNEY: ...Jennifer.

CHRISTINE: Oh.

BONNEY: The muck-spreader insinuates... (*Bitter laugh*) It's so obvious you must've guessed.

CHRISTINE: No.

BONNEY: What's the first thing that comes to mind?

CHRISTINE: Sorry.

BONNEY: Christine. Think.

CHRISTINE: I am thinking.

BONNEY: (*Irritation*) Then think harder. (*Christine thinks but shakes head in negative*) Christalmighty! Do I have to spell the sodding thing out? (*Christine just stares at Bonney*) That Jennifer and me... that our relationship is more than professional.

CHRISTINE: Oh that. I thought of that ages ago.

BONNEY: You did?

CHRISTINE: Of course. But it's so 'jealous-wife', I didn't think it right to say.

BONNEY: Absolutely. It's lame. Lame, and obvious and... how they think they can get anywhere with lies like that is beyond me.

CHRISTINE: I don't know why you pay it any attention. It's a natural thought to have...

BONNEY: It is?

CHRISTINE: I've had it hundreds of times. But I say to myself, Christine, either you trust him or you don't. If I didn't I'd go mad with suspicion...

BONNEY: You would?

Music starts up again.

CHRISTINE: Good god, yes. Could build up an Everest of distrust where you and Jennifer are concerned.

BONNEY: Based on what?

CHRISTINE: Use your imagination. (*They begin to dance again. This time a quickstep. Bonney imagines*) Why did you bother?

BONNEY: What?

CHRISTINE: To tell me?

BONNEY: They might try first. I don't want any nasty surprises. If you're ready for it, if you meet it without a blink, it's stillborn.

Jenner approaches. Taps Bonney on shoulder

JENNER: If I may.

BONNEY: Very quaint George.

CHRISTINE: Such a gentleman.

BONNEY: (*To Christine*) ...Finish our chat later.

Christine and Jenner dance. He's a bad dancer. He doesn't move with her, he stumbles, but they manage passably well

CHRISTINE: Thought you'd forgotten me.

JENNER: Would I? Could I?

CHRISTINE: Now, now.

JENNER: What?

CHRISTINE: There are limits.

JENNER: Then don't stare at me.

CHRISTINE: Do I?

JENNER: Stare me right in the eye. Stop me dead. Make me wonder. Could she...? Would she...? And it all comes roaring back.

CHRISTINE: That's enough James. It's too late and I'm too old to start switching partners, even if I was madly in love with you, which I'm not. And if I stare at you, and I'm not sure I do, it's because I'm interested in people in general, and for no other reason.

JENNER: Good. Go on. I want you to crush my hopes. I want to know I'm an idiot. Don't leave any doubt I'm imagining things. If you're totally firm, it'll help. This is the second time I've... we have to put a stop to it once and for all.

CHRISTINE: Don't I know it.

JENNER: From this moment, the subject is taboo.

CHRISTINE: Good.

JENNER: Now I know, categorically, I've no chance, I feel relieved. I can come to terms with the role, position and dignity of friend. I was never happy making up to you behind James' back. I felt double deceitful. Well, now, admittedly through none of my own choice, I won't be doing it anymore. I'm a grateful man. In fact you've shamed me into admitting that I, yes I have accidentally helped to...

CHRISTINE: Is James popular?

JENNER: Very... Spread that mali...

CHRISTINE: Disliked?

JENNER: By some.

CHRISTINE: Hated?

JENNER: Strong word – hate.

CHRISTINE: But true?

JENNER: At this present difficult period. Passions are roused. Tempers high. The battle lines drawn...?

CHRISTINE: Accusations made? (*Jenner nods assent*) The more scandalous the better? Are both sides equally bad?

JENNER: Good god, no. We're not like them... normally.

CHRISTINE: Times aren't normal.

JENNER: Even so... we might spotlight the odd gaff... political machination.

CHRISTINE: But not personal?

JENNER: Not unless it were mega damaging – candidate a paedophile child-abusing alcoholic, hopelessly dependent on stealing from Primark. Have to eliminate Achilles heels before the opposition swoops. (*They start to dance again. Christine gingerly avoids Jenner's feet*) Of course, that being so, as I was about to say, I myself have been guilty... in some measure...

CHRISTINE: Shush George. I need to think.

James dances on stage with Jennifer.

They approach Jenner and Christine.

Through the next lines of dialogue both couples dance in reasonably close proximity.

BONNEY: We meet again.

JENNIFER: Hi.

CHRISTINE: Hi.

JENNER: Hiyerr.

JENNIFER: I dragged him on.

BONNEY: She dragged me on.

CHRISTINE: He could do with the exercise.

BONNEY: The fight against flab. (*Pause while they dance around*) My eye on you.

JENNER: Nose-ache.

BONNEY: You bet.

JENNIFER: If you don't watch us, we won't watch you.

BONNEY: Sounds exciting.

CHRISTINE: Shall we swap?

JENNIFER: Oh no. He's mine. (*Holds him to her*)

BONNEY: (*Embarrassed*) Trapped I'm afraid.

CHRISTINE: I shall sulk.

Bonney and Jennifer start to move away as they dance.

JENNIFER: By-ee.

Bonney and Jennifer dance off stage left. Christine and Jenner dance on, for her part mechanically.

He treads on her toe, again. Quite hard. She stops, rubs bruised toe.

JENNER: Was that a toe?

Christine walks to small round table downstage left. It has two hard chairs round it. She sits. Jenner follows, sits in other chair.

CHRISTINE: They make a good couple. (*She takes foot out of shoe, massages toes. looks at James & Jennifer dancing*)

JENNER: As I was about to say...

CHRISTINE: ...Almost clings. Almost familiar.

JENNER: People do... when they dance. (*Jenner looks at Bonney and Jennifer*)

CHRISTINE: I'd never dance with you like that.

JENNER: Oh no, Chris', no. If you're thinking...

CHRISTINE: (*She looks again*) Good god! She kissed his ear.

JENNER: No. No I think you're wrong.

CHRISTINE: She tickled his ear with her tongue. I saw it.

From now to end of scene Christine doesn't, for one moment, take her eyes of Jennifer and Bonney.

JENNER: Larking around. I might do that to you at a party...

CHRISTINE:	You most certainly would not. My god, if I thought…
JENNER:	Chris, I don't think there's anything between them.
CHRISTINE:	Why did you say that?
JENNER:	Because I… well I…
CHRISTINE:	I never mentioned it.
JENNER:	It was obvious what you were thinking. And it's totally ridiculous. Put it out of your mind. You've got to, d'you hear?
CHRISTINE:	Very keen that I do George. Incredibly keen.
JENNER:	No, I'm not. Not incredibly. Just ordinarily. Sorry if I sounded O.T.T. I just think you're wrong.
CHRISTINE:	And the more you go on, the more suspicious I'll get you're covering up.
JENNER:	I won't say another word. You're too sensible to… (*She looks at him. He shuts up*) They're waving. They want us over there.
CHRISTINE:	We'd better join them. So I can keep a closer eye on them.
JENNER:	You don't need to do anything of the sort.

Christine and Jenner stand. Exit SL

END OF SCENE

SCENE EIGHT

Rose's flat. A week later.

Kate dressed in leotard, exercising to rock cd.

Enter Rose, laughing in disbelief. He switches Kate's music off.

ROSE: Ha, ha, ha! I don't believe it. Ha, ha, ha, ha... (*Kate continues exercising*) Listen to this...

KATE: D'you mind?

ROSE: No, you must. Just listen. (*He reads from his mobile*) 'The burglar has filled his sack. He mustn't escape with the swag'. Ha, ha, ha, ha. 'Swag'. Who the shit uses the word 'swag'? Oh the elegance of the prose, the power of the imagery. Your father should've been a poet. Ha, ha, ha, ha.

KATE: You're spoiling my exercise.

ROSE: I mean if anyone's stolen the 'swag' it's your father. This parliamentary seat is what he's stolen! I really do wonder if I was at the same meeting when I read this. He has true genius. It's called factual-distortion with imaginative flair.

KATE: Don't do that.

ROSE: What?

KATE: Please don't frown. You look old when you frown.

ROSE: No, but really. What d'you think?

KATE: I think you've got a damn cheek marching in here switching my music off. I want to exercise.

ROSE: Don't you think he's wonderful? I mean just read that and tell me if he isn't totally beyond the pale.

Holds out mobile so Kate can see screen.

KATE: Well... s'ppose it's one rung in the moral ladder above spreading rumours.

ROSE: Meaning what?

KATE: You know.

ROSE: I'm sorry I do not.

KATE: Meaning my father is not having an affair with Jennifer like some people would have us believe. How could you stoop so low?

ROSE: Kate... now listen Katiekins, you're stirring your placid, even-tempered Malkie up. I've had nothing to do with any muck-raking or slander that may be flying round this or that committee room or bar where Labour members meet. It's not my thing. I don't indulge. I never have. I focus on what's wrong with James politically. The rest is a distraction.

KATE: It isn't to me. It's my mother and father...

ROSE: I understand. It wouldn't be to me if it was my father being accused of doing that to my mother. But I'm not James' keeper am I? I can't sort it out. Maybe you can. I'll ignore what you just accused me of. I won't even ask what sort of a person you think I am that you could even think that of me. I'll ignore all that and tell you it's a horrible situation and I feel for you but I can't let it take me over. My focus is on James as an MP. (*He slaps paper*) That's what's important to me.

KATE: My Dad's a good father and he's been faithful to Mum. And I love him. It's horrible to hear such lies.

ROSE: Then ignore them. I do. Or try to. They don't move us forward. Politically. In fact they bog us down in people's bloody private lives. And you can't build a progressive movement dissecting people's private lives.

KATE: God knows what I'd do if it were true. I'd... kill her. I'd tear out her hair and punch her and...

ROSE: Your father's private life's a bloody distraction. Yes it is Kate, it gets in the way. But that's the problem. I can't get you to see your father objectively. The minute I try, ever so gently by the way, to criticise him, you leap to his defence. I've failed miserably in getting you to see that it's his politics I don't like, not your dad as a person.

KATE: Oh shut up, shut up, shut up!

ROSE: Exactly. You've just proved my point.

KATE: Submerged in politics. Drowning in politics. Destroyed by politics.

ROSE: Is that so? You know do you?

KATE: When I first met you, at the Christmas fund-raiser for refugee children, I thought what a pleasant young man. Not a bastard, not how Dad described you. You weren't the same person. Couldn't be. You talked about literature, fairy-cakes, the white elephant stall. You were interesting and charming and considerate to everyone. Now it's all strategy and tactics for advance and what's the enemy up to and how can we counter them. You think of nothing else.

ROSE: You're so so wrong! I've got one other passion outside of politics. Shall I tell you? Do you want to know? My other passion is for a shapely young woman in a leotard.

KATE: Knew it all along. You want me for my body. Not even my body, just a body, so long as it has the right holes and wears a leotard.

Rose advances to Kate and takes her hand firmly in his

ROSE: Now there I draw the line. At making love to a body. An unattached trunk. A faceless torso. Horrific.

KATE: That's what you just said.

ROSE: My other passion is for sexy Kate Bonney in a leotard.

They kiss. He lies on top of her. She pushes him off, lies on top of him.

KATE: Better?

Rose pushes her off. They struggle. He gets on top once again.

ROSE: I like it like this. (*He bends to kiss her. Just as he does, she throws him off, and gets on top of him*) Devious with your sexual positions? Two can play at that game.

KATE: Apologise for disturbing my routine.

ROSE: I humbly apologise.

KATE: Promise not to again.

ROSE: I promise. (*Rose expects Kate to kiss him now. She doesn't*) I'm waiting.

KATE: What shall I do? About Dad? Mum's worried. She wouldn't have mentioned it otherwise.

ROSE: Christ, do we have to?

KATE: Yes, we do. (*Pause. Serious*) Is it true?

ROSE: I honestly don't know, and short of spying on your Dad I'm unlikely to find out.

KATE: He wouldn't be so cruel. I mean poor Mum.

ROSE: Can't you forget it? Just for now. Here and now? And think about us instead.

KATE: I'm sure it's not true. Dad'd never do anything so horrible to Mum.

ROSE: If you want to know who's spreading the story I can tell you.

KATE: Of course I want to know.

ROSE: George Jenner.

FADE DOWN ON ASTONISHED KATE

END OF SCENE

SCENE NINE

Park.

Bonney and Christine walk.

CHRISTINE: Things can't go on like this...

Bonney squats down looking across pond.

BONNEY: Look at him. He's a beaut'! (*She doesn't*)

CHRISTINE: For the past three weeks you've been out every night of the week.

BONNEY: Here boy. Cheepy-cheepy-cheep.

CHRISTINE: You were supposed to cut down on engagements. Jennifer said she'd see you did. Hah! She seems to encourage you to do the opposite with no regard for your health. Whenever I mention it to her she lets me know what a fuss-pot she thinks I am. Are you listening?

BONNEY: Of course I'm listening my love.

CHRISTINE: You're overdoing it.

BONNEY: I do as much as I have to.

CHRISTINE: You look tired and unhealthy.

BONNEY: Compliments, compliments.

CHRISTINE: You were given a strict regime and you're not keeping to it. You drink too much, you smoke, you get no exercise.

BONNEY: So peaceful here...

CHRISTINE: And she's to blame.

BONNEY: Who?

CHRISTINE: Her.

BONNEY: Jennifer?

CHRISTINE: Yes.

BONNEY: Not Jen'. She's totally bloody efficient.

CHRISTINE: Let's not be modest. She's superwoman. She cooks, drives, organises, teaches. And all for you.

BONNEY: Chris'. The little devil jealousy.

CHRISTINE: She makes me feel a failure. She makes me feel I'm not looking after you. I can't stand it.

BONNEY: Put it out of your mind. (*Standing for the first time*) What has got into you Chris'? (*No answer*) She's no competition. She's work. (*Pause*) You can't blame her for my mistakes.

CHRISTINE: Sack her.

BONNEY: Are you serious? (*Chris nods negative*) What the hell for? What reason? Well? There must be a reason? Preposterous! Can't even give me a reason.

CHRISTINE: How dare she dance with you like that?

BONNEY: Like what?

CHRISTINE: All over you...

BONNEY: Once a year?! Both full of drink?! I'd just told you about the poison spreading, you obviously started imagining things...

CHRISTINE: Tickling your ear. Kissing your neck.

BONNEY: I don't remember.

CHRISTINE: I'm telling you.

BONNEY: Oh really. Sack her because you can't control your fantasies? And what about her? Have you thought about her? What she'll do if I sack her?

CHRISTINE: I'm worried about what she'll do to us if you don't.

BONNEY: Don't tell me you think the rumour's true?

CHRISTINE: I'm not happy and she's the cause, that's what I think.

BONNEY: Not happy about what?

CHRISTINE: Sort it James. Or I'll sort it for you. One way or another. (*She strides off*)

BONNEY: What d'you mean? Chris'? Christine.

Bonney hurries after her.

LIGHTS DOWN

END OF SCENE

SCENE TEN

Bonney's house. Living-room.

Enter Christine and Kate.

KATE: ...Thought you'd like to hear the news, in person.

CHRISTINE: Oh yes. Of course we would. Oh well done, Kate, well done.

She takes a letter out of a shoulder-bag

KATE: 'Dear Miss Bonney, we are pleased to inform you that – subject to minor corrections – your thesis on the Impact of NGO's in the Developing World has been accepted for the award of Doctor of Philosophy'.

CHRISTINE: Dr. Bonney. Is that what we call you?

KATE: In public. In private I'll let you call me Kate. As a favour. As you've been good to me. In fact I'll still treat you and Dad as equals, in private. (*Pause*) Is he in?

CHRISTINE: No.

KATE: Know when he will be?

CHRISTINE: No.

KATE: No idea at all?

CHRISTINE: None.

KATE: Ah. (*Pause*) Will you tell him? When you see him.

CHRISTINE: I don't.

KATE: Don't what?

CHRISTINE: See him. We don't have a 'seeing' relationship anymore. We've a strange hybrid consisting of infrequent phone-calls and the occasional scribbled message! (*Pause*) He's probably round hers. The number's there. (*Points to phone*)

KATE: He won't slam down the phone on me?

CHRISTINE: He won't pick it up if he's otherwise engaged. Y'know – the position he's in, the ecstasy-level at the precise moment the phone rings, whether he can reach the receiver without stopping the action...

KATE: Mum. You shouldn't...

CHRISTINE: My new dark sense of humour.

KATE: Not exactly side-splitting is it?

CHRISTINE: I need more practise. (*Pause*)

KATE: Mum what's happened? What's he done?

CHRISTINE: Knowing his tendency for self-indulgence, just about everything.

KATE: You don't think...?

CHRISTINE: I do. I hired a car and followed him... hoping it'd all be suspicion and nonsense. They go back to hers when he says he has meetings.

KATE: You don't know what they do.

CHRISTINE: She clings to him like a leech. (*Switch*) I've made up my mind. I shall force it out of her.

He's got no right to humiliate me for that little trollope, little tart... little slut! She's a selfish person who doesn't give a thought for anyone but herself. It shows what he's become — that he can spend five minutes with her and not find her objectionable. She probably gets down to him if he looks bored. When I think... how possessive he was after his heart-scare, how demanding... wanted me, clung to me! Like a kid sometimes... too much sometimes. I don't know him anymore. He doesn't know himself, he's in such a corner. Up and down, enervated, betwixt and between. Constant movement and absence of thought are what keeps him functioning.

KATE: Apart from her clinging, and the going back to her place, you've not actually seen them...? (*Christine stares at her*) Can't he get a new secretary? (*Christine nods her head in negative*) Have you suggested it?

CHRISTINE: Yes. A number of times.

KATE: When will you see her again?

CHRISTINE: Soon.

KATE: Let me be there. It'll be stronger with the two of us. We'll ask her to resign her job. We'll explain that it may not be her fault but for our peace of mind would she please disappear from the scene.

Christine sits down. Kate walks up to her. Puts her arms round her shoulders comforting.

CHRISTINE: I'll be alright. I'll talk to her. Thanks for the offer. You're a sweetie.

LIGHTS DOWN

END OF SCENE

SCENE ELEVEN

Jennifer's house

Lights up on Bonney and Jennifer on sofa. From their position & mood they look as if they've made love.

BONNEY: Christ, I wish I hadn't… we hadn't. In the first place. That was the moment, the crunch. Not that it was bad. Good god, no. It was good. Best thing that's happened to me in years. Best selfish thing. Not sorry I did, just wish I hadn't.

JENNIFER: I wish I hadn't too.

BONNEY: Of course you do. (*Pause*) Why?

JENNIFER: Because you're older than me…

BONNEY: More mature.

JENNIFER: …And you've got a family who think a lot of you. (*She gets up. puts a night-gown on*) I'll help you pack.

She moves off stage left. Bonney gets up, starts to dress. Jennifer returns with a briefcase and hold-all.

BONNEY: God, you're right. It's bloody childish. Make a mess of my life.

JENNIFER: And others'.

BONNEY: And others'. I've been rotten selfish. No I haven't. Fairly selfish. All my life. Now I have to change, to be one hundred per cent considerate or we're going to have an upheaval…

JENNIFER: (*Gathering Bonney's odds and ends together*) I resign my post.

BONNEY: Um?

JENNIFER: As your secretary. I won't see you again and that way temptation is removed.

BONNEY: (*Finishing touches to clothes*) You're right. That's a sensible, necessary and admirable step. You'll be hard - no impossible – to replace, but it's got to be done. (*Bonney busies himself cramming his 'things' into his two suit-cases*) This is right. The right thing to do. Dump the past. Crush the sodding rumours.

JENNIFER: What rumours?

BONNEY: Oh… just rumours…

JENNIFER: About what? Or can I guess?

BONNEY: Can you?

JENNIFER: You and me…?

BONNEY: Bullseye. We're the scandal of the moment. Everyone's talking about us. It's so useful in the fight to weaken me. (*Switch*) I decided to tell Christine – shit-scared they'd get to her before I did, and ever since she's been in a filthy mood. Wanting me to sack you, blaming you. I've no room for manoeuvre.

JENNIFER: Who put it round?

BONNEY: Who knows? Neither of us I presume? (*Looks at her hard*)

JENNIFER: Is that meant to be funny? (*Telephone rings. Jennifer picks it up*) Yes he is. (*To Bonney*) It's George.

Bonney moves to phone with haste spotlight on Jenner on one side of stage. We hear clearly what he says.

JENNER: ...Trying to get you everywhere. Tried this number in desperation.

BONNEY: Must be important.

JENNER: Good news. Could give you a second life.

BONNEY: Go on.

JENNER: Been scrutinising the new members list. Bit of a fluke really. Almost a technicality...

BONNEY: What?

JENNER: A number of them break the three month rule. Really explosive one is Park. There's definitely two iffy ones there. We lost Park by one vote. It could've given us at least a tie – Chairman's casting vote, you'd've won.

BONNEY: Fantastic. I prayed for this. Dreamed about it. We'll tell the National Executive. I lost by a whisker and in that situation one vote in a local ward can alter the balance right through. If we can get a re-run, with the support we've got now we'll stuff 'em.

JENNER: I've got the names here. All Rose clones.

BONNEY: Good work George. My place. Eight o'clock.

Bonney puts phone down. Jenner does same. Spotlight off Jenner. Bonney prays.

> Ineligible voters. Manna from heaven. An upsurge of local opinion is good. The support of my Parliamentary colleagues is better. But proven illegality tops the bloody lot. (*He does a little skip for joy*) Praise the lord for illegal voters. Lets have hundreds of them, and all Rose supporters. (*He flops back into sofa, elated*) Well done George. What a demon. What a friend. (*Pause*) I hope he's got it right... Has to a definite breaking of the rules.

Jennifer is standing with a briefcase in one hand and a hold-all in the other.

JENNIFER: Your shirt's undone. (*Bonney looks. Button on waist undone. He buttons it up*)

BONNEY: Ugly old fat, look't it! Brighton or the Cote d'Azur?

JENNIFER: It's your luggage. (*Bonney takes briefcase, puts it under arm. Takes hold-all in hand of same arm. They stand close, facing each other*)

BONNEY: I'll post your wages.

JENNIFER: Fine.

BONNEY: Well...?

JENNIFER: Well?

BONNEY: I um… (*He puts the hold-all down. Then the brief-case. He takes her hand in his, draws her towards him*)

JENNIFER: Memento?

BONNEY: Something like. (*They kiss*) Bye Jen'.

JENNIFER: Bye James. (*They kiss again, passionate*)

Bonney breaks away, holds both her hands in his.

BONNEY: Sod it, why should I?

JENNIFER: Because you sneak off here, you sneak back there.

BONNEY: I don't sneak.

JENNIFER: How d'you think I feel?

BONNEY: If you'd got bogged down in previous relationships it was too painful to throw off and I loved you enough, I'd be patient.

JENNIFER: Why don't you tell her? Aren't you sure?

BONNEY: Jen'.

JENNIFER: You're not or you would. You like it this way. The interlude-screw, the bit on the side.

Bonney puts down hold-all. Holds out briefcase ingratiatingly

BONNEY: Can I interest you in our latest range of sex-aids, madam? (*Takes out his electric shaver*) For the woman with the older man. The new vibraphone vibrator. Aerodynamic shape for ease of entry. Natural oscillation. Replaces

>   tired limbs and extends worldly pleasures in ways never dreamed of before.

Jennie's unmoved. She walks to a sideboard. Picks up a diary. Hands it to Bonney.

>   You're not serious? Alright, have it your way. You don't like sharing, we'll stop. Secrecy's a bore, we won't. I'll move in with you. We'll go public.
>
>   So what if I destroy my career? Ruin my home life?
>
>   So what? We mustn't inconvenience you must we Jen'? You're the only person in the world who counts.

Pause

JENNIFER: Your wife rang me.

BONNEY: What for?

JENNIFER: A chat.

BONNEY: About what?

JENNIFER: The situation. She intends seeing me sooner or later.

BONNEY: Make sure you're not in.

JENNIFER: Jen' the disappearing woman...

BONNEY: You can see why.

JENNIFER: Less and less.

BONNEY: Christine could hurt me. I can't afford any steamy revelations – not now. Not this

	moment. (*He collects hold-all and briefcase again*)
JENNIFER:	...I'll go on lying then.
BONNEY:	Just for now.
JENNIFER:	(*As Bonney walks to exit*) You'll type out my lines?
BONNEY:	You simply say it's a smear with no substance...
JENNIFER:	I do?
BONNEY:	You have to. For my sake. I need time. I need breathing space. I need a clear run through the next few months. Till I've got this vote sewn up. Once that's over it'll be nigh on impossible to get rid of me. Then we'll go public. Please Jen'. Just for now?
JENNIFER:	You always get your way. I always give in. I must idolise you. What other explanation can there be?

LIGHTS FADE

END OF SCENE

SCENE TWELVE

Local party offices. Small room.

Enter Rose and Kate.

ROSE: There's a chair in there. I'll leave the door open.

KATE: You're surely going to tell Dad I'm here?

ROSE: Yes, yes I will. (*Holds door open for her*)

KATE: Do I have to? This is silly.

ROSE: I want you to hear him. How he operates.

KATE: Two minutes. Then I'm in.

Kate exits. Rose sits on hard chair.

Enter Bonney

BONNEY: ...We know where we stand and why, so lets dispense with preliminaries. I've called you here for a chat.

ROSE: Jolly decent of you old chap. Honoured I'm sure.

BONNEY: You're finished. Your little cabals, alliances. The devious way you work. It's all to no avail. We've scrutinised the voters. Two members in Park Ward weren't eligible. (*Rose shifts away*) The constitution states a member may only vote after three months continuous membership.

ROSE: Inclusive or exclusive?

BONNEY: Um?

ROSE: Do we include the day they joined? Do we take it from midnight of the day, or noon, or the exact second, they put their signature on the card? Or perhaps the Party has its own astronomical time-scale – a digital quartz system conforming to the movements of the solar system. You're pathetic. The way you squirm. The way you ferret out devices to save your face. Two members have been in the Party a day less than required and your lot scream illegal.

BONNEY: The two in question gave those on the GMC who wanted me to face a vote of no-confidence, a majority of one. Without them you'd've lost Park and lost the vote. (*Rose turn on heel and strides to exit*) Wait! An olive branch. Or we'll both lose. Chew each other up and let someone else in. Tell them – your momentous Momentum Opus - if you come out strongly for me continuing as MP, withdraw your no-confidence motion, put a stop to rumours about my private life, I give you my word I'll graft to get you adopted for another constituency. I'm in a position to know when vacancies arise. I can put in a good word. I further promise to support you on the local council and to cease all attacks on you and your supporters in the press.

ROSE: You still don't understand.

BONNEY: Understand what?

ROSE: That we want your support on local issues *and* in Parliament. That you need to push for a left-wing alternative in both areas - something you never do.

BONNEY: Let's hear these alternatives.

ROSE: Stop committing to privatise everything in sight.

BONNEY: It works.

ROSE: I could've saved my breath.

BONNEY: Don't give up so easily. Anyway there's hardly anything left to privatise. Our economy is privately owned lock stock and profitable barrel.

ROSE: We still have a National Health Service.

BONNEY: Just...

ROSE: Work to keep it publicly owned.

BONNEY: I'll work to get the best value for money...

ROSE: Sell it to privateers to make mega profits you mean?

BONNEY: If they give the best service...

ROSE: But they do. To their shareholders. Welcome to your brave new world of no-fail capitalism. Ladies and gentlemen, did you think making a profit carried a risk? Did you think risk-taking defined it? Well think again. Gone are the days when you might actually go bankrupt. The new contracts are rock-solid blue-chip because they're government backed. Failure in business isn't an option. Making a profit very much is. And the profits are vast. Beyond your wildest dreams. Profits whose fertile soil is the need for every one of us to eat, to drink, to shelter from the storm and stay healthy.

Kate enters from next room

KATE: Hi Dad.

BONNEY: What are... where've you been?

KATE: Next room.

BONNEY: For how long? What for? What're you doing there?

KATE: Waiting for Malcolm.

BONNEY: Are you... spying on me? Did he set this up?

KATE: No. Don't be silly.

BONNEY: A recorder job is it? In your bag? On your phone? (*To Kate*) You'd do that to me?

KATE: I've not done anything of the sort. Why are you accusing me of such horrible things? Malcolm was meeting you so I waited in the next room...

BONNEY: Without saying hallo? Quiet as a mouse? Not my daughter. She wouldn't do that. (*To Rose*) Turning her into your spy are you?

Bonney raises finger and points it at rose. Looks horrified at Kate.

Bonney exits

ROSE: Did you have to walk in just then?

KATE JUST STARES

LIGHTS DOWN

SCENE THIRTEEN

Jennifer's flat

Bonney lies spread-eagled on sofa.

Jennifer listens to voice-recorder (tiny) of Bonney asking.

Questions in the house.

BONNEY: ...Is the Health Secretary aware of these allegations?

Does she intend, in the light of them, to outsource NHS contracts to a company with a proven record of inefficiency and mismanagement, not to say suspected dishonesty?

POLITICIAN'S VOICE: We are aware of certain statements made regarding the conduct of...

We hear a great burp across the recording. Jennifer switches off.

JENNIFER: I can't believe you did that.

BONNEY: Wind.

JENNIFER: Such a brilliant point. Wrecked because you couldn't control your bodily functions. (*Front door bell rings. Bonney freezes*)

BONNEY: Who the hell is that?

JENNIFER: Not Christine I hope.

BONNEY: Christine? Why the hell would it be Christine? Did you know she was... shit and sod it!

Bonney exits upstairs. Jennifer opens front-door.

Enter Christine. She walks in SL, turns and stares at Jennifer.

CHRISTINE: I know he's here.

JENNIFER: He often comes to...

CHRISTINE: Screw? (*She walks stage left, shouts upstairs*) James! Don't skulk. Come out and show yourself.

James clatters down stairs breezily.

BONNEY: Hi Chris'. Not skulking, my love, studying. Come in. Take a seat. Tea? Coffee? Wasn't expecting you. Last person I expected. Just sifting some papers, away from the din. Something alcoholic? 'G&T'? Sherry? Jennifer? (*Jennifer nods her head in negative*)

CHRISTINE: Tell me James, is it her youth that's so powerful? Or the fact she sticks to you like a limpet?

Walking up to and around Jennifer

Is this your reward for being an MP? A beautiful young woman who panders to you? Flatters you, makes you right all the time? Is that what it took to make a fool of you? Is she a twenty four hour a day paid-up member of the superior skivvy club? Does she write poems in praise of you, exaggerate what you've achieved, pretend you're still young? Or does she have more intimate points that keep you panting along behind? Is her fanny tighter than mine? Does she do things I won't do – though I'm pretty broad-

	minded when it comes to sex? Whatever it is, d'you think it'll last once she's got you?
BONNEY:	Chris you're all arse-upwards on this.
CHRISTINE:	(*Screaming*) Don't lie! Can you please not lie? Just this once? Can you spare me that? (*Silence*)

Christine calculates her effect.

> How could you James? Be so cruel?
>
> How could you lie to me and make such a fool of me? After all the years I've been faithful to you? (*To Jennifer*) This is all your fault. James can't see it, but we know, you and me. You planned it from the day he took you on. I've watched the way you work. You're much too shrewd for poor, silly, James. He's like a lumbering, great, emotional, elephant compared with you. Beneath the sexiness and the style you're razor-sharp. God, what a… reward, what a horrible surprise. I'm very, very hurt. I feel like killing both of you here and now but I'd have it on my conscience for as long as I live and you're not worth that.
>
> (*To James*) I'll take you back. I'm an idiot I know. I've told myself I shouldn't, but I have to think of you James. You'd go to pieces without me. It may not seem like it now, but you just think of the future. You're twice her age. Superficially she's attractive. In five, ten years' time she'll be praying you drop dead,

because she'll have another man in her sights. A younger man. And with her morals the temptation will be much too strong. And you James will be left stranded in old age and you can't cope with being alone. I know. You can't go one evening without needing someone to wipe your bottom. So. We're all allowed one idiocy, especially public men who are too soft with camp-followers. Are you ready?

BONNEY: I was just this minute coming...

CHRISTINE: Immaculate timing. Tell this person you'll never see her again.

BONNEY: I can't see the point of...

CHRISTINE: Tell her I said!

BONNEY: Alright. If that's what you want but I feel for Jennifer.

CHRISTINE: When you say things like that I want to hit you. I want to sink my nails into your face...

BONNEY: Alright okay. (*To Jennifer*) I won't see you again.

CHRISTINE: (*After a pause. To Jennifer*) You're dismissed. As from now, you no longer work for my husband.

JENNIFER: That's not for you to say.

CHRISTINE: James?

BONNEY: Yes. (*To Jennifer*) Sorry Jen'. I can't see any other way...

Jennifer stares at Bonney, who avoids her look. Bonney and Christine exit.

FADE DOWN

END OF SCENE

SCENE FOURTEEN

Party offices

Corridor. Bonney and Jenner walk down it.

BONNEY: So the vote of no-confidence goes to a full members' meeting?

JENNER: There's not been enough time for the NEC to disqualify it.

BONNEY: (*Arm round Jenner's shoulder*) But you think we'll win?

JENNER: I've done the maths and I think we should.

BONNEY: The first steps down recovery road. We're on course for the double. I've had a boost. Shadow junior spokesman on Voter Registration. In the re-shuffle. JC's just told me. He may be left-of-left and he has to go but in the meantime he knows a talented moderate when he sees one.

JENNER: Jeremy reaching out to the middle ground?

BONNEY: God help him. I'll be well placed to bring my party back to what it was before the Corbynistas overran us.

JENNER: Devious bastard aren't you.

BONNEY: Difficult times require exceptional behaviour.

JENNER: Junior spokesman eh.

BONNEY: You're the first to know.

JENNER: All we need now is to win an election.

BONNEY: And we can. With people like me in positions of influence. England needs surgery not butchery despite what JC and his left-wing vandals think. I'm good with a scalpel. A professional. A bit of an artist I like to think.

JENNER: If it wasn't for it being butchery, I wonder if you might be thinking of lopping your own leader's head off?

BONNEY: Even the finest surgeons are subject to the occasional slip-up. (*Wink*)

JENNER: With bloody results ha ha.

Rose is seen approaching with Kate. She stops by her father. Rose walks on a few steps.

KATE: Hi Dad.

BONNEY: Did you speak?

KATE: Can I just say well done?

BONNEY: Do you dare?

KATE: Dad, please.

ROSE: Don't bother Kate's a waste of breath.

BONNEY: And you can hold your lip. You're behind this.

ROSE: Do I throw up now or do we leave? (*Rose moves towards stage right*) Are you coming?

BONNEY: Go on, take her. I'm sure she'd rather. (*Rose exits*) One down...

JENNER: I'll wait outside.

Exit Jenner

KATE: I'm glad you got that appointment Dad. Really glad.

BONNEY: That so-called democrat wants me destroyed. And you show your loyalty by not only going out with him but forming a political alliance with him.

KATE: You do things I don't like. Doesn't stop me loving you.

BONNEY: I've never willingly given you pain Kate.

KATE: And Mum? What's that then? Pleasure?

BONNEY: Spare me please. Pure imagination. She must've sat at home with a bottle of booze, encouraging every insecurity she ever had to run riot.

KATE: So you haven't...

BONNEY: Of course I haven't whatever you thought I had. Yes, they're may've been a wheensy grain of emotion not strictly within professional boundaries, but good god where isn't there? And what harm is it? Your mum and I are old enough to cope with hiccups like that.

KATE: Everything's alright?

BONNEY: Stop cross-questioning me. It's you who should be explaining your actions to me

	because Kate, you've hurt me deeply...that spying business. I feel betrayed... attacked...
KATE:	I wasn't spying. Since when do people spying walk into the room where the person they're meant to be spying on, are? And I'm not against you – I happen to love Malcolm, that's all.
BONNEY:	That puts you against me. It boosts his morale, and lowers mine. (*Longish pause. It sinks in*) You could help me. Yes. If you were serious. You could work on Malcolm to withdraw his no-confidence motion. Tell him about my sleepless nights, my arrhythmia, my fingernails bitten to the quicks! (*He flashes his fingers*)
KATE:	Dad.
BONNEY:	My health has deteriorated – fact. Family activities've gone down the pan because I've no time for them – fact. You can talk him out of his anti-me policy, because you're close to him – fact.
KATE:	Alright...
BONNEY:	You will – you'll talk to him?
KATE:	Yes.
BONNEY:	Promise?
KATE:	I promise.
BONNEY:	When? Tonight? (*Kate nods*) And you'll phone to let me know how it went? (*Kate

	nods. *Again Bonney hugs her quickly*) That's my girl.
KATE:	I... never got that job by the way.
BONNEY:	What job?
KATE:	Full-time lecturer. My college. They decided to keep me hourly paid.
BONNEY:	How could they? Idiots. It's their loss – you're better than them Kate. Poor kid. Don't worry. Let me buy you a drink. You can tell me all about it and then we'll work out how to defeat Rose's Red Army.
KATE:	Malcolm's waiting for me...
BONNEY:	Let him wait. (*He ushers her out upstage left*) If you can swing this one for Daddikins you're a saint. I'll never breathe a word of criticism. You'll be my bestest, favouritest loveliest girl again.

Bonney exits with Kate.

Enter Jenner after a few moments.

He looks around – no Bonney.

Enter rose from opposite side.

JENNER:	The birds have flown. Not a good day for you Malcolm. By my calculations you'll lose the no-confidence vote.
ROSE:	Unlike the careerists of the right, we on the left know how to take defeat with honour.
JENNER:	Fancy a drink?

ROSE: I won't give up the fight. Not even full of beer.

JENNER: Suspicious bastard aren't you?

ROSE: Mainly with people I know.

JENNER: Call it my perverse warm and friendly side that's inviting you for a beer. Nothing more than that.

ROSE: On those terms I'll join you. I'm not sectarian when it comes to sharing a drink. (*They exit together*)

LIGHTS DOWN

END OF SCENE

SCENE FIFTEEN

KATE & MALCOLM'S FLAT

Malcolm sits in front of computer.

Kate looks at screen over Malcolm's shoulder.

ROSE: (READING) 'Rose you are a snivelling left-wing ponce. Your days are numbered. Watch how you cross the road comrade.' Ha, ha, ha, this one's going to run me over.

Kate clicks off email and into new one.

KATE: 'I hate you reds. You ought to fuck off back to Commie Land! We're going to see you don't cause any more trouble round here!' (*Rose laughs*)

ROSE: I've never been so famous. Everyone's tracking me. Everyone wants a chunk of me.

KATE: People are so crude and petty and disgusting. I know what you think Malcolm but Dad doesn't like this. He's just as upset as you.

ROSE: He's not physically violent I give you. He just creates the atmosphere that breeds it. Badgering his band of right-wing journos so the message gets out. What a victim he is, how my followers – that's you – threaten him on social media, troll him with abusive comments and it's all total bloody lies, invention and exaggeration. Result – local members we never see to talk to, think I'm a political thug as well as a moral defective, not to say an outsider, not to say a man

	inspired by a malevolent foreign creed that's against the glorious British way of life.
KATE:	Say the public was listening to you? What would you say about him?
ROSE:	Where's my dictionary of insults?
KATE:	This is affecting him.
ROSE:	Having to drink more is he?
KATE:	Sarcasm is the lowest form of wit…
ROSE:	…But the highest form of personal comment. Everyone leaves that bit out.
KATE:	Dad's supposed to avoid stress.
ROSE:	Maybe he should stop messing around with younger women then.
KATE:	That was blown up out of all proportion.
ROSE:	You've changed your tune.
KATE:	I've talked to him about it. (*Rose looks at her sceptically. Kate responds with a defiant glare*). Let Dad get on with his job. Work another way. I'll talk to him. Tell him to listen to you.
ROSE:	You know what I think? Your father uses you. He's using you now. Did he ask you to speak to me?
KATE:	No. (*Pause*) Yes.

ROSE: Never misses an opportunity. And he's suddenly going to listen to you? When he's home and dry you mean?

KATE: Alright, he uses me. I'm still worried he'll overdo it and give himself another heart-attack only this time a fatal one. And I don't want him to die... because he's my father and I love him.

ROSE: I won't back down. And the more bricks come through that window...

KATE: Has someone thrown a brick?

ROSE: Figuratively I meant...

KATE: For a horrible moment I thought someone had.

ROSE: ...Can you stop interrupting?

KATE: Can you stop worrying me?

ROSE: ...And the more insults I get in my Inbox, the more people attack me on twitter, the more determined it makes me.

KATE: Oh brave. You're so fucking principled aren't you? How does it feel to be so deeply, in the right? D'you feel like a knight in armour? Or is it more the Jesus Christ tradition? How d'you cope with the stigmata – bandages or Elastoplast? How'd'you bridge the gulf of superiority that cuts you off from the rest of grotty mankind?

ROSE: It's very difficult but I manage.

KATE: You allow nothing where my father's concerned. You bark out ultimatums you think I should give him as if he were a bloody stranger. You've never once considered, or even recognised my feelings for him.

ROSE: You've got to choose. He's making you.

KATE: You see everything from your own point of view.

ROSE: It's 'with me or against me' with your father.

KATE: You've done nothing but attack and criticise him ever since we met...

ROSE: I criticise him *politically*.

KATE: ...Having a go at me as if I'm responsible for what he does. You don't want me with him, you get jealous like a child. You have some mad idea he controls me. Can't you accept I control my own life?

ROSE: Five minutes with him and Kate as an independent being has scarpered – enter Kate the adoring daughter who thinks Daddy's the axis of the universe.

KATE: So jealous. So paranoically jealous. And so totally wrong.

Pause

ROSE: If his health is that bad why doesn't he jack it in? I don't wish your dad any harm but I can't stop fighting for what I believe in because he's not super-fit. (*Switch*) Alright I

	admit it - I am jealous when you're with him. He hates my guts. He's totally justified no doubt but it makes me anxious because what's he telling you when I'm not there? It's not nice for you but I can't be 'laid back', I can't let things slide. I might lose you. I don't want to.

They embrace. Warm. Comforting. Tender.

	If you think he's at risk tell him to have time off.
KATE:	He tells me what he wants me to get from you. You tell me what you want me to get from him.
ROSE:	I'm not asking you to get anything from him.
KATE:	Yes you are.
ROSE:	If you threaten me with his death how d'you expect me to respond?
KATE:	Just shut up! Bridge that gap. To and fro. Tell him this, tell him that! You both use me. You both judge me by what I can do for you. How loyal I am to you.

Longish pause

ROSE:	Don't say a word to him then. If you dare say a word to your father now...
KATE:	Stop ordering me about! Who'd'you think you are anyway?

ROSE: Don't accuse me of using you. I'm effing well not... (*He's rendered speechless*) All I'm doing is seeing if you're as committed as I am.

KATE: Stop attacking my father.

ROSE: Stop talking about him then.

KATE: You started it.

ROSE: You mentioned him first.

KATE: Because you implied he was behind this hate campaign. (*She picks up emails they've printed*)

ROSE: We'll agree not to talk about him ever again.

KATE: I'll give you five minutes...

ROSE: Taboo. I promise.

Pause. They both smile.

KATE: Love you.

ROSE: And I love you.

They nuzzle.

FADE DOWN

END OF SCENE

SCENE SIXTEEN

Parliamentary office of Bonney.

Bonney is sitting at desk working.

Door opens, enter Jennifer, with carrier.

Bonney doesn't move.

JENNIFER: I will sit down. (*She sits*) Saw you on telly. You were good. Just right in fact. Confident without arrogance. Articulate but not beyond the common man.

BONNEY: Jen'.

JENNIFER: Brought back memories. I know that person. We have unfinished business.

BONNEY: You shouldn't've come.

JENNIFER: (*Handing over carrier*) I scratched round for an excuse and... your things. Some of them anyway.

BONNEY: I can't see you.

JENNIFER: The rest are rotting at home.

BONNEY: Christine's paranoid. My position's changed.

JENNIFER: So has mine. And not to my liking. You haven't phoned, haven't written, nothing. I keep thinking he'll get in touch soon, it must be soon. He's got a plan.

BONNEY: How can I explain? (*Gathers himself*) Imagine I'm a climber. There above me lies the summit. It takes effort, and guts, and luck to reach it, but if I persevere, one day I might. The way is full of danger. At any stage I could lose my footing through lack of judgement. I could shout too loud and start an avalanche that'd bury me for good. I could rush ahead and find I'm exposed to the elements with no back-up team to get me out. And then the inner temptations. When the going gets tough, and the summit's obscured in mist – the voices that tempt you to let go, relax, fall into the next crevasse. I did fall once but I stuck out a foot and halted my slide. Next time I might not be so lucky.

JENNIFER: You've never climbed a mountain in your life. You can't stand on a chair without vertigo.

BONNEY: An extended metaphor Jen'. For my life.

JENNIFER: I'll extend it further. D'you want a back-up team that's young and fit and full of daring, or one that sits comfortably at base-camp advising you to come down before you catch cold?

BONNEY: Switching teams half-way up could lead to disaster.

JENNIFER: Switching metaphors would put me out of my misery. This one's naff.

Bonney feels in his trouser pocket. He takes out some money in notes.

BONNEY: Please. Take it. Three months wages in advance. I got it ready for... Pathetic I know but what else can I do?

Jennifer doesn't take it so he stuffs it into her shoulder-bag.

JENNIFER: I could get hooked on this.

BONNEY: You'll have to leave. Or I'll have to.

She takes off her coat, crosses her legs.

No temptation. I'll show you out.

Bonney walks round to her side of table

While I'm still in control.

He picks her coat off back of chair. Raises her with one arm. Fumbles her coat on. They end up by door, close to each other.

Love that bloody perfume.

JENNIFER: I thought you did.

BONNEY: I do. It's...

JENNIFER: Will you come for the rest of your things? (*Bonney nods slowly in negative*) I'll dump them. (*Bonney puts his arms round her. she pushes him off*) I mean it – the papers you left. The briefs... The personal info'. Send it sailing into the street.

BONNEY: When? Christ, I shouldn't. We know I shouldn't.

JENNIFER: I'll be in all night. Tonight.

BONNEY: If you have it ready. I'll just pop in...

JENNIFER: As quick as you like.

They embrace, kissing passionately.

Door opens, enter Christine.

CHRISTINE: I was just…

She sees them. Stops short.

Oh my god!

LIGHTS DOWN

END OF SCENE

SCENE SEVENTEEN

Open-air degree presentation ceremony. Lots of people.

Rose and Kate stand. She has full academic regalia on—gown, mortar board. We hear names being called out.

ROSE: So the issue is clear – do we have elected representatives, subject to the will of the rank and file of the Party, or do we have a team of political super-stars who work by their own cabalistic rules and rituals, the most fundamental of which is that, once elected the right to interpret the will of the people is conferred upon them and them alone?

KATE: Full stop?

ROSE: Semi colon. That is the essence of the battle between me and your father. I am Sir Galahad; he, the evil Prince. I've got bigger muscles. I'm obviously more likeable...

KATE: The subject is taboo.

ROSE: Given this clear moral choice, will the Party be brave enough to move to dump James, or will a veil of double-talk, innuendo, and personal smear swamp any movement for change?

KATE: You're breaking our agreement.

ROSE: And so to my final comment on this afternoon's critique of James Bonney, M.P. – he's a man who wants to take the party I love in a direction I detest, that is a betrayal of everything we stand for... (*He sees James approaching*) ...oh and as he's right now heading this way, I'm pissing offsky.

KATE: But you'll miss my moment.

ROSE: View it from a different angle.

KATE: Bloody hell... Malcolm come back. Will you please come here?

Exit rose. We hear voice droning on with names in background

Kate follows after him.

Enter shortly Bonney and Christine.

BONNEY: ...Why your eyes are so red...

CHRISTINE: The wind.

BONNEY: There isn't any. We need an explanation.

CHRISTINE: Not me. You. I'm not explaining. You explain. You did it. You... you...

BONNEY: Worthless, rotten, bastard?

CHRISTINE: And worse. Not having the guts to stick to what we agreed. Allowing her to do that in front of me? I've never been so humiliated in all my life.

BONNEY: I did stick to the agreement. That was the first time I'd seen her since before. I didn't ask her to visit. She bloody well turned up. How could I stop her?

Christine looks as if she's about to attack him.

CHRISTINE: Aaaaaaagh!

BONNEY: Ssssssh! People are staring. (*Christine plonks herself down on the grass*) Chris', get up. At once. Chris for goodness sake. (*He starts to pull her up, smiling at people around him every now and then. Then very loudly...*) That ankle again. What a pain. (*Quietly to Chris*) Here comes Kate. Get up will you. (*Loudly again*) I'll have a look. Tendon is it? Where does it hurt? (*He bends down to look at ankle. To Kate*) Trotsky's gone to ground I see.

KATE: If you mean Malcolm...

BONNEY: Not his sort of 'do' – all this pomp & ceremony.

KATE: What name was that? I lost it. (*We hear the name 'Brown' over the sound system in the background*) Oh now I've missed being called. Oh what a disaster. Dad why can't you be quiet? I'll have to tell them.

BONNEY: Don't trip over.

Kate runs off to formally accept her degree award.

CHRISTINE: Bastard. You.

BONNEY: Calm down please.

Christine is distraught. Bonney looks around uneasily

CHRISTINE: After all you promised. After all we said. You are beneath contempt. Your morals would pollute a sewage-farm. I have never met anyone who cared so much for himself and so little for everyone else.

BONNEY: (*Side of mouth*) Of course I care.

CHRISTINE: Then why did you do it?

BONNEY: She puts a spell on me.

CHRISTINE: You dare blame her! You dare have the brass-necked cheek to blame it onto her!

Kate re-enters. Angry.

KATE: I've been put back to the end. (*She looks in puzzled way at her mother*)

BONNEY: Kate I'm really sorry. Your mother and I will have to leave. Mum's twisted her ankle.

Christine weeps bitterly to herself. Bonney looks around frantic to preserve appearances.

For god's sake can we go?

Kate bends over mother, solicitous.

KATE: Mum. You alright? (*Arm round her shoulders*)

Slowly Christine stands.

CHRISTINE: What have I done to deserve this? The times I could've slept with a man. The chances I've had. (*Raising voice*) I've had thousands of chances to sleep around. I could've opened my legs to half a borough.

Bonney places his arm under hers and shepherds her along.

BONNEY: We're going home.

CHRISTINE: Let go of me you bastard! Let go!

Bonney lets go. Christine shouts to people around her.

	This man, this Member of Parliament, can't get enough fanny! He's pussy-mad!
BONNEY:	Can you stop…?
KATE:	Mm please stop.
CHRISTINE:	Lock up your daughters or he'll have their knickers down before you can shout 'canvass'. Especially the young ones. A flutter from a youthful eye-lash and he's a ravening lech. A quick pout knocks his morality for six. A flash of thigh destroys any self-restraint he pretends to have.
BONNEY:	Shut up for Christ's sake Chris'!
KATE:	Let's go somewhere quiet Mum.

He starts to tug her along again.

CHRISTINE:	Remember his face! Member of Parliament, Islington Central. Shadow spokesman on voter registration. Look at it! The face of a lech! A cheat! A liar! (*Bonney slaps her round face. She immediately slaps him back, even harder. And again. And again*)
BONNEY:	I'll wait by the car.
CHRISTINE:	Not for me, you won't! Not for me! Wait where you sodding well like but you won't wait for me. I don't ever want you waiting for me, ever, ever!

Bonney looks at Christine, then turns on heel and leaves. Christine is crying. Kate cuddles her tenderly.

KATE:	Don't cry, Mum, please don't cry.

FADE DOWN

END OF SCENE

SCENE EIGHTEEN

Some days later. Christine at home. She's beautifully made up. We see her drink a glass of whisky, then another. She looks drawn, but still attractive ring on door. Exit Christine.

Enter Christine almost immediately with Jenner.

CHRISTINE: Come in.

JENNER: O.K.

CHRISTINE: Sit there. (*Indicates sofa*)

JENNER: What here?

CHRISTINE: No, there. (*He sits on sofa*) Drink?

JENNER: Please

CHRISTINE: Have a whisky?

JENNER: ...Just a taste.

She pours him a big tumbler full.

CHRISTINE: Not seen you for weeks.

JENNER: No.

CHRISTINE: Ignoring me.

JENNER: Yes... I mean no.

CHRISTINE: You mean yes.

JENNER: I mean no. Busy, busy, working my socks off. James has been energy itself. No confidence vote looming. Meeting after meeting to save James' skin. Life's all action-replay with one difference – this time I think we'll win.

CHRISTINE: It's the thought of her finger poking him in the ribs. He daren't slow down. But we won't talk about that. Tonight's our night. We're going to drink, and chat, and let our hair down. I'm not D.I.Y'ing, or digging gardens, or cooking dinners. Dumped in a ditch... learning to climb out. (*She stops near Jenner*) George, you've not touched a drop. (*Jenner sips. Christine swigs freely*) Get it down you. We may not be twenty but we can still sparkle.

She plonks herself on sofa next to Jenner.

I know how you feel about me. I always have. At the time I couldn't respond, though I was flattered, but now I can. I'm free. After all this time I'm free. Liberated. Giving myself to you.

Jenner stands and moves away, serious.

JENNER: I can't

CHRISTINE: You can't?

JENNER: I can't.

CHRISTINE: Why not?

JENNER: I just... can't...

CHRISTINE: (*Pause*) Oh you mean...? Oh dear. I never realised. (*Pause*) Have you been like that for... well always?

JENNER: Like what?

CHRISTINE: You know. Unable to. Incapable of...?

JENNER: Oh god. I don't mean I can't because *I can't*. I mean I can't because I don't feel like it.

CHRISTINE: You don't?

JENNER: I'm not silly. You're not doing it out of love for me. You're doing it for revenge.

CHRISTINE: No I...

JENNER: You are Christine. I know.

CHRISTINE: You're very perceptive all of a sudden.

JENNER: I'm very right.

CHRISTINE: So what if it's true? Does it matter? Who cares about motives? Who knows them?

JENNER: I tried to tell you once, at the annual dance that... well it was me that started the whispers... about James and Jennifer.

CHRISTINE: Who cares?

JENNER: Not in a calculating way. I don't think in a calculating way. I was angry he hadn't turned up to the umpteenth meeting. So I let it slip. 'He's knocking off that secretary no doubt,' I said it more than once. I knew it would spread like wildfire. I'm an old hand.

CHRISTINE: I don't know why you want to tell me this. It's done. It's over. You did people a... you did me a favour.

JENNER: Was it just a slip of the tongue? Or did I hope it might help me with you? Did I want to fan the flames in the hope that you'd hear, or he'd tell you?

CHRISTINE: If it has helped you've a strange way of showing it. My God you've a delicate conscience.

JENNER: You still don't fancy me, and I couldn't lay a finger on you knowing that.

Christine looks hard at George.

A certain realisation strikes her about him. She suddenly relaxes.

CHRISTINE: Affairs are no big deal. I could've if I'd wanted. I decorated instead. Why couldn't he have mown the lawn? (*She reflects*) I feel I've been dumped in the bottom of a very rank and slippery pit. I've lost my bearings. I'm drowning in muck. My mouth full of dirt.

She gulps her drink, then spits it out wipes mouth violently with hand. Slight vomit. And again, and again. Jenner sits, embarrassed. Gradually she recovers.

       'S better. I feel better now.

Fade down on Christine and Jenner sitting on sofa looking ahead.

END OF SCENE

SCENE NINETEEN

Bonney lies on floor. Jennifer sits over him on sofa.

BONNEY: So. I've jumped. In the rapids. No going back. No second chance. I'm swimming for my life. Got a flutter in my stomach, my mouth's bone dry. Kate's grown-up, independent, an adult. Chris' is resilient. When the shock dies down I'll get in touch. I see no reason why we can't be friends.

Pause

Marriage isn't forever. Not now... not in the modern world. You have to move with the times. There was a Prime Minister of Iceland was a single mother. Questions've been asked about bachelor Heath. John Major was shagging Edwina Curry in the cabinet office. Regularly. Lloyd George was an over-active Welsh ram. It didn't hold them back, so why should it me? Providing it's sensibly handled. No one being silly. Making a fuss. Broadcasting it.

We switch to another area of the stage.

Christine Bonney is in a public phone booth. She dials.

CHRISTINE: ...The Guardian? I have a story. James Bonney, MP, shadow spokesman on voter registration, and his secretary Jennifer Allen have been found in a burning flat. Contact Westminster police for further details.

She puts phone down. Dials again.

> Could you send a fire-engine to 241 Selwyn Gardens, S.W.1 immediately! The flat is on fire. There are people inside whose lives are in danger.

She puts phone down. Walks to stage area representing flat where Jennifer and Bonney lie arm in arm she sets fire to a 'Guardian', stuffs it through letterbox. Then another. Then another.

JENNIFER: I won't live in Christine's shadow. If you give your love grudgingly you can forget it.

BONNEY: Is that a threat?

JENNIFER: It's how I want us to be. An equal pair. Matched. One day a family...

Christine puts a match to yet another newspaper.

The fire spreads.

BONNEY: I begrudge you nothing.

Bonney and Jennifer kiss. Lie side by side.

JENNIFER: I'm happy.

BONNEY: Me too. It's a new beginning.

JENNIFER: I shall organise you so well... the meetings, the travel, the functions. You won't waste a minute. (*Bonney sniffs. And again*) We'll work hard... I'll make sure you do. I'm going to push you till you get a proper shadow cabinet post

BONNEY: Can you smell something?

JENNIFER: ...Not junior spokesman on voter registration... something bigger... more prestigious.

BONNEY: That's smells like... burning... (*He stands, walks to door, views flames licking up inside of front door*) Jesus Christ the place is on fire. (*They both start to cough*) Through the corridor!

JENNIFER: It's ever so hot.

BONNEY: I know who did this. I bloody well know! She wants to kill us.

JENNIFER: Soak a sheet and wrap it round.

BONNEY: Right.

Exit Jennifer stage right to kitchen.

Feet. What about our feet?

Fade down

Fade up

Jennifer squats in corridor outside flat. We see a wet sheet Bonney comes into view.

BONNEY: She's already called them. They're on their way.

JENNIFER: Takes care of everything doesn't she?

Bonney surveys flat.

BONNEY: Listen. It was an accident. You were having a smoke. You fell asleep. Newspapers caught fire... I wasn't here...

Enter Christine behind. Christine sits down very near to Jennifer.

CHRISTINE: You were. I smoked you out. In the commission of your crime. Against the married state.

JENNIFER: I know you're angry Christine but this is getting dangerous.

CHRISTINE: I've phoned the papers. The great publicity machine you're so fond of.

We hear a police siren off.

JENNIFER: It's nothing to be proud of.

CHRISTINE: Proud? Of behaving like a criminal? Destroying things? All my life I've created. How could I be proud?

We hear voices, shouts and footsteps offstage as of fireman and others arriving at speed.

FADE DOWN

END OF SCENE

SCENE TWENTY

Kate's & Malcolm's flat

A few days later Christine, at table, sorts through a pile of newspapers. They're neatly stacked.

Enter Kate and Rose, carrying boxes of leaflets.

CHRISTINE: ...It's as if it never happened.

Kate and Malcolm reluctantly take newspaper Christine thrusts into their hands. Christine turns back to a letter she's writing.

> 'Dear Sirs, I protest. You have suppressed the truth.' – my hook. 'I attempted, in cold blood, to murder my husband and his secretary yet I'm charged with nothing. When James Bonney says a cigarette fell and caught his Guardians alight, he's lying...' Read on dear. (*She hands paper to Kate*)
>
> (*To Rose*) How's the Party? Riven to its moral bone? Muttering darkly in all corners?

ROSE: You've got star-billing right now.

CHRISTINE: Good. Will James lose support?

ROSE: I really don't know.

CHRISTINE: You ought to.

ROSE: I can't see why. Not on this.

CHRISTINE: My dear boy, seize every opportunity.

ROSE: It's not an opportunity, it's a distraction

CHRISTINE: From what?

ROSE: ...Political issues of greater importance.

CHRISTINE: That's not the way I see it.

ROSE: It's a massive and mucky red herring and the sooner it's over the...

KATE: Malcolm, help me tidy these away please.

He walks to Kate. Looks into one of the three carriers. Takes ream out and places on floor near wall.

CHRISTINE: I've told the Head. She was speechless. A failed murderess on the staff? 'Mrs Bonney, your previous misdemeanours pale into insignificance beside this latest event. Think of the school. Think of the pupils. Young children are too fond of matches and fires without finding a role-model in their teacher. For as long as you're here, I won't feel safe. I'll live in constant fear of flames licking round my well-formed – some would say obese – limbs. Not even your husband's reputation can save you now.

KATE: Mum. This isn't helping. Can you stop?

CHRISTINE: He threw me into this cess-pit but I kept hold of his hand.

KATE: Watch out you don't destroy yourself just so you can destroy Dad.

CHRISTINE: Dear Kate, you want to help but you don't understand. You don't see what moves me isn't spite or revenge but self-respect. I simply can't stop till the poison's out. Shall I make us a nice cup of tea?

Exit Christine in to kitchen.

Kate and Rose reflect.

ROSE: I'm never getting married. (*Pause*)

KATE: It's not just married people who have crap relationships.

ROSE: If your parents weren't married... (*He pauses*)

KATE: Yes?

ROSE: ...It'd probably be just as bad.

KATE: Thank you.

Pause. Each in own world.

ROSE: I still won't. Not even if I become an MP. Not even if they put pressure on me to.

Kate walks up to him. They hug. After a bit.

How long's she staying?

KATE: As long as she wants.

ROSE: Well, how long's that?

KATE: I don't know. Maybe a week, maybe a month. I daren't leave her alone for a minute.

ROSE: Oh right, right. I don't particularly want her living with us but I see what you mean. She's

	having a tough time. We have to help her. As much as we can.
KATE:	Still love me?
ROSE:	Don't be daft.
KATE:	Do you?
ROSE:	If we're equal, and we say we are, you can't ask that.
KATE:	Why not?
ROSE:	Because it puts me above you.
KATE:	Why does it?
ROSE:	You're giving me the power to say yes or no.
KATE:	What's wrong with that?
ROSE:	It should be understood that we both love each other equally, no question.
KATE:	Oh. Right. I won't ask.
ROSE:	Right then.
KATE:	Never ever?
ROSE:	Not if we're solid.
KATE:	Do you though?
ROSE:	Do you love me?
KATE:	Yes. You me?
ROSE:	Yes.

They kiss. Door buzzer goes.

KATE: I'm not expecting anyone.

Exit Kate. Sounds of talking off. Kate returns with Jenner.

                    I'll help Mum make tea. (*Exit into kitchen*)

JENNER: Still friends?

ROSE: Absolutely.

JENNER: I know politically we haven't always seen eye to eye – but we're both reasonable men. We're ready to give the odd inch when it's needed. We're not into sodding hysterics.

ROSE: Sounds like me George.

JENNER: Between you and me he's impossible. If there was a wrong time to risk having his private life turned into a local scandal he's chosen it. The man's off his head. Stark, staring mad. Does he want to bloody lose? I've had enough! Working my balls off for him and all he does is shit on me from a great height. I mean he only had to be a bit sensible for fuck sake.

I'm an agent. If you ever take over, I'll work with you. What I'm saying is, I won't resign. If James is ousted... provided you're reasonable that is... provided there's no take-over bid by the Fourth International. Like we don't have to learn the sayings of Trotsky by heart.

ROSE: I trust that's heavy-handed irony?

JENNER: It wasn't serious.

ROSE: I'm a democratic socialist, like my leader JC. I'm no Trotskyist. You on the other hand haven't always been so sure of your political home.

JENNER: My membership goes back many years

ROSE: Your Communist Party one goes back further.

JENNER: Indiscretions of youth... isn't that what we say? We ex-reds?

ROSE: The bureaucrat-vampires are out for blood – left-wing blood. If they don't get their fix they die. You label me a Trotskyite – even as a joke – you're offering up my jugular.

JENNER: No more jokes. Like I say – if you're reasonable, if it's moving your way – fine, provided it's not nationalising the crown jewels and my local pub...

ROSE: As you said James, I'm a reasonable man.

JENNER: Pleased to hear it, Malcolm.

ROSE: But the crown jewels belong to the people...

JENNER: Now who's joking?

ROSE: What d'you think James' chances are?

JENNER: He's squandering his personal credit. Where is he? No one's seen him for weeks. The vote's in a few days. Your side could win...

ROSE: So we stand a chance?

JENNER: Better by the hour. Despite the fact most members still love James.

ROSE: If I could win this vote it would be a boost. A first small step to a transformed party in parliament – a party to change things.

JENNER: Let's get you in first.

ROSE: That's essential.

JENNER: Y'know... I was thinking... if you and Kate got married we could say we'd kept it in the family.

ROSE: I've got no plans to marry.

JENNER: I wasn't being serious.

ROSE: Jokes are out remember?

JENNER: Pity. This whole business has been one big joke from beginning to end. (*Lights down*)

END OF SCENE

SCENE TWENTY ONE

Bonney's flat. Evening. Two days later enter Bonney. Looks unhealthy, short of breath.

BONNEY: (SINGING) 'You got to get at 'em. Get up and get at 'em. That's what to do!'

Enter Jennifer.

JENNIFER: Lie down. At once. (*Bonney lounges in sofa, propped up by arm at one end*) That's not lying. (*She undoes his shoes, takes them off, and loosens his tie. Takes his jacket*)

BONNEY: Anyone would think I was an invalid.

JENNIFER: I'm calling a doctor.

BONNEY: You are not. I'll take my pills. (*Exit Jennifer*) In the egg bowl. (*Enter Jennifer with pills, glass of water. Hands them to Bonney. He drinks*)

JENNIFER: How bad is it?

BONNEY: It's not bad. It's average. Give me a drink, it'll disappear. Give me two I'll forget I ever had it.

JENNIFER: If you want a drink you can have water.

BONNEY: Hard-water area. Imagine your arteries furred up like the inside of a kettle.

Exit Jennifer

Bonney takes drinking flask out of briefcase, has good swig. Puts it back looks around brightly. Sings.

> 'Here I sit, alone in the wilderness,
> 'lone in the wilderness,
> 'lone in the wilderness,
> Here I sit alone in the wilderness,
> I haven't had a drink all day!'

Holds chest in pain.

BONNEY: Bloody indigestion.

Re-enter Jennifer with tray of tea-things but no teapot. She sits on floor by Bonney. She holds his hand tenderly. He strokes her cheek.

JENNIFER: Next week we're going away for the weekend. A whole two days... We're going to laze, forget everything. Have you been to Lulworth Cove? It's a perfect circle, a suntrap, and there's a funny little caff' right by the beach. (*Bonney brings out whisky flask*) Give!

BONNEY: You mean this? (*Indicating whisky flask*)

JENNIFER: D'you want to die?

BONNEY: No one's beaten it so far as I know Jen'.

JENNIFER: No need to invite it in sooner than you have to.

BONNEY: I don't. I ignore it.

JENNIFER: That's no good either. Follow a routine. Be careful. Be sensible! (*Pause. Bonney strokes her cheek. She relaxes again*) Give up unnecessary activities. Give them all up. Take time out. I'll keep us I promise. I need

	you healthy. (*Pats tummy*) We need you healthy.
BONNEY:	You'll keep quiet about that won't you?
JENNIFER:	Not a word till you say go.
BONNEY:	When we're out of the tunnel and we nearly are. I'll win on a sympathy vote. Lets face it, a fallen middle-wayer's better than a pure young upstart. I've kept a lid on the fire business... Christine was overwrought... imagining things. Jealousy got hold of her. (*Boiled kettle pings in kitchen*) Brothers and sisters, ladies and gentlemen, I stand in front of you, a humbled man, a better man, more than ever ready to serve your interests. Give me your vote, I'll give you an arm and a leg.

Exit Jennifer into kitchen.

Bonney holds his chest again.

The pain forces him to stand up.

        Angina regina.

He staggers a few paces.

        Jen'. Jennifer...

He calmly lies down on the floor. He curls himself up womb-position. Jennifer enters.

JENNIFER:	James? (*She runs to him*) James, what's the matter? James, say something!

BLACKOUT

END OF SCENE

SCENE TWENTY TWO

Kate & Malcolm's flat.

Next morning. Malcolm strides up and down, agitated, watching BBC news.

NEWS: (*Newscaster reads on TV*) ...The departure of Ms Eagle brings the number of ministers who have quit Jeremy Corbyn's shadow cabinet to eighteen...

ROSE: (*At TV*) ...Backstabbing feckless egotists...

NEWS: ...Hilary Benn's sacking is now seen as the spark that lit the fuse...

ROSE: He sacked himself you slippery BBC bastards! If you tell your leader you've lost confidence in him you give him no choice.

NEWS: ...It is felt to be simply a matter of time before Mr Corbyn himself resigns...

ROSE: (*Shouting at TV*) Don't you dare JC! Stay or socialism's fucked for another fifty years.

NEWS: ...Breaking news just in. Gloria de Piero, shadow minister for youth, has resigned...

Rose gets up, walks to TV, shouts at it.

ROSE: Treacherous careerist! High-heeled assassin! GMTV poster girl! (*Look at watch*) Hold on. Just a sec' ...one an hour... on the hour... metronomically? Malcolm you tosser, you fool, you idiot. It's a coup... a carefully-planned anti-JC coup!

Enter Kate with two bags of shopping.

KATE: ...I've just heard the most upsetting news.

ROSE: (*Shouts at TV*) ...Bomb every country that steps out of line abroad! Assassinate your newly-elected leader at home!

KATE: Jennifer's pregnant.

ROSE: Is she? Did she announce it as the clock struck one?

KATE: Sorry did she what...?

ROSE: ...It's what Labour Party careerists do. Dish out bad news on the hour to inflict maximum damage.

KATE: It's certainly had a bad effect on Mum. She's distraught. (*Hands him anonymous letter*)

ROSE: (*Reading aloud*) 'Jennifer Allen is pregnant. It's right you should know.' (*Turns letter over*)

KATE: Mum got it this morning. She phoned Dad. Jennifer answered. Dad wasn't taking calls. He'd been advised to avoid stress. Yes she was pregnant. Yes James was the father. She hoped Mum was pleased for her.

ROSE: James. What a role-model eh. How to create the perfect trail of human wreckage as you journey through life.

KATE: ...Fancy not letting Mum speak to Dad. How hard is that? (DOOR BUZZER SOUNDS) That'll be Mum.

ROSE: Am I supposed to know this stuff?

KATE: I'm sure that's why she told me to leave her to park. So I could tell you.

Kate exits back into hall. After short while kate re-enters with Christine.

CHRISTINE: Hi Malcolm.

ROSE: Hi Christine.

CHRISTINE: Hope you can stand me for another evening.

ROSE: Pure pleasure Christine.

CHRISTINE: I'll pretend you mean it.

ROSE: If I say it I mean it.

CHRISTINE: Nice. To be treated with respect. Which you always do Malcolm. Makes me feel vaguely human. Did Kate tell you?

ROSE: Tell me what...?

CHRISTINE: ...Did you darling? The latest twist. I bet you were expecting it – a sharp observer of people like you.

ROSE: It's not something I...

CHRISTINE: I'm a bit emotional. I must be strong. (*To Kate*) Come away with me Kate? A holiday... like when you were a child. Do us good. You too Malcolm.

ROSE: Thanks for the offer...

KATE: I have to find a job Mum...

CHRISTINE: Somewhere warm and exotic. 'S more fun with two... or three.

Malcolm's mobile rings.

ROSE: (*Phone to ear*) Who? I'm tied up right now... (*Mouths to Kate & Christine*) It's George. Can he pop in? News. (*Helpless gesture*)

CHRISTINE: I'm always pleased to see George.

KATE: (*Quietly*) ...If he must.

ROSE: (*Into mobile as he exits*) I'll buzz you in. First door on left.

Exit rose to hall. Buzzes Jenner in.

CHRISTINE: (*Slight pause*) ...When I set fire to James's flat...

KATE: ...Tried to set fire...

CHRISTINE: ...I didn't want to kill him. Not definitively. I love him too much.

KATE: Mum...?

CHRISTINE: It was more wanting to let him know. And her. You can't treat me like this. I won't stand for it.

KATE: Well... no one died, you weren't charged so all good.

CHRISTINE: People understand. That woman's wrecking my life. James's too if he's not careful. The insatiable demands of youth. He kids himself he's up to it but he's not. His next heart-attack may be his last.

Sound of front door opening off. Muffled voices in conflab in entrance hall.

CHRISTINE: George? Is that you? Come and say hallo to your favourite wronged wife.

Enter Rose and Jenner.

JENNER: Evening Kate. Christine how are you?

CHRISTINE: I'm not sure George. Not sure at all to be honest. How are you?

JENNER: I came with news but Malcolm says you know already.

CHRISTINE: You mean the 'royal' pregnancy?

JENNER: See – my news is stale.

CHRISTINE: I thought I had you to thank for telling me. (*She rummages in handbag*)

JENNER: ...Me?

Kate hands letter to Jenner. He reads.

CHRISTINE: This isn't from you?

JENNER: If I'd written it I'd've signed it.

CHRISTINE: Not you in your 'man-of-the-shadows' mode?

JENNER: If something needs talking about I'll talk. Not send anonymous letters.

CHRISTINE: Now I've no idea who my mystery friend is. (*Waves letter*) Are you eating with us George?

JENNER: I couldn't...

CHRISTINE: It's no trouble.

JENNER: Well if...

CHRISTINE: Chicken liver risotto. James's favourite.

Exit Christine into kitchen.

KATE: So who told you George?

JENNER: What?

KATE: The news.

JENNER: Oh it was um... someone... John...?

KATE: ...Or George or Paul...?

JENNER: John Deal I think.

KATE: Who told him?

JENNER: Don't know. Didn't ask.

KATE: People knew before Mum did – John Deal, the letter-writer... Either Jennifer prattled on about it or Dad trusted someone he shouldn't have. (*Stares hard at George*)

JENNER: (*To Malcolm*) ...Any chance of a chat?

ROSE: Chat away.

JENNER: Well I... well it's... (*Looks at Kate*)

ROSE: Kate and I share everything.

JENNER: Please don't think this is anti-James, Kate. It's not. It's... politics.

KATE: So it's going to be unpleasant and sordid. I'm sure I'll enjoy it.

JENNER: (*To Malcolm*) This pregnancy can move things your way.

ROSE: Going to stop shadow ministers jumping ship like myopic rats?

JENNER: With more MP's like you in parliament yes.

ROSE: And how will that happen?

JENNER: You make it happen. You get stuck in! Now. Ditch the moral high ground. James is window-dressing his private life for his own benefit. Caring husband with problem wife. Lie upon lie and getting away with it because members don't challenge him... including you.

ROSE: Including me bollocks. I have nothing to do with it.

JENNER: Malcolm you need to learn one thing and learn it fast. *The personal is political.* James is out of sight when it comes to this. He paints you as a cocky young upstart who can't laugh at a joke and who looks down your nose at everyone. A) it's personal, b) it's untrue and c) it's effective – it turns members off you.

ROSE: I want to win the political battle. If it takes time so be it. The victory will be sweeter.

JENNER: Say it takes so much time there is no victory. If you want to have any chance of being MP for this constituency copy your enemy. Fight dirty.

ROSE: I won't fight over the sores of James' private life.

KATE: No and you won't need to. Jennifer can't hide her pregnancy forever. The more obvious it becomes, the more members will see what Dad's been up to.

JENNER: By the time that gets round to all the members – if she doesn't refuse to say who the dad is – James'll be home and dry.

KATE: She didn't refuse this morning when Mum rang.

JENNER: Will you listen to my plan? (*Pause*) You 'n me write a letter. How much we've admired James as a person and politician – his fine record as local MP. Now we find it's a fantasy based on lies. His lies. Especially about his highly-strung and jealous wife. We are saddened by James' behaviour. We feel such a man can't be trusted to carry on as our MP. I dig out as many James-haters among the party locals as I can, get them to send this letter to everyone who's anyone – local papers, affiliated bodies, the world and his dog – anonymously if need be. If we do this we'll damage James. It's a campaign with no comeback *on* you but a lot of benefit *to* you.

KATE: Malcolm wouldn't dream of getting involved in such a horrible business would you Malcolm.

JENNER: You'd boost your chances. You the man of principle, *rose*-balm on the party's wounds.

ROSE: I wouldn't feel comfortable...

KATE: Of course not. It's sordid.

JENNER: Then let James win! Let him lie about his family life. Let him slander poor Christine, say the most hurtful untrue things about her. And let his political ideas win too. Because one thing's certain – if he wins, so do they.

KATE: Why are you so keen on getting rid of Dad, George? You've been his loyal agent for years.

JENNER: The way he treats our local Party. The way he treats your mother.

KATE: That didn't start today. Why the change of heart?

JENNER: When an MP acts in the...

KATE: D'you fancy my mother George? Is that it? Your chance to be Sir Lancelot riding to her rescue on your white charger?

JENNER: I respect Christine more than anyone...

CHRISTINE: (*Off*) I can hear every word in here. It's fascinating.

JENNER: ...But I know she loves James...

CHRISTINE: (*Pokes head round door*) I do for my sins. Sorry George.

JENNER: No that's... fine. Maybe it's this – I'd rather work with people who behave well than people who don't.

KATE: But you've just suggested a campaign using anonymous letters from vetted members that they didn't even write themselves. What's behaving well about that?

JENNER: Spreading the truth among party members can't be behaving badly.

ROSE: Yes but I mean… a letter written by us but signed by others as if it's come from them…?

KATE: All to make Dad look badder than bad.

JENNER: We can only make him look bad if he's doing bad.

CHRISTINE: (*Entering room*) And he is. Very bad. You can't say he isn't Kate.

KATE: I'm not going to but it sticks in my throat when George acts the saint. His reasons for doing this are as self-interested as anyone's. And that's why Malcolm won't give it the time of day will you Malcolm?

ROSE: …It's crucifying to think James could win this vote on a pack of lies.

CHRISTINE: (*To Kate*) James doesn't think twice about treating me appallingly. Why shouldn't Malcolm dish him out some of his own medicine?

JENNER: It's your call Malcolm. Say the word, I'm ready to start.

KATE: Don't dare say any word of any sort.

JENNER: Win this vote or lose it. It's in your hands.

KATE: No Malcolm.

CHRISTINE: Losing this vote may make James value things. Precious things. Like me for example.

JENNER: Well Malcolm? We're waiting? What's it to be?

All eyes on Malcolm.

ROSE: We need to win... that's what counts... bright ideas, progressive actions... what I'm focused on... and nothing else.

LIGHTS FADE

END OF SCENE

SCENE 23

Crematorium. Exterior

Enter Kate and Rose.

ROSE: Great. So personal. Did you see the priest? He could hardly keep awake. Zipped through the effin' service at ninety miles an hour, a few prayers, half a hymn and off rolls your solid pine coffin to an unknown destination behind velvet curtains. Sod all that. All those hangdog faces. I want a socialist burial. 'The family of man / Keeps growing...' Quotes from my favourite authors. Everyone nicely tanked. Good food. You're alive. I'm dead.

KATE: Was it my father?

ROSE: Where?

KATE: In the coffin.

ROSE: Highly probable, but you never know one hundred per cent.

KATE: I never saw him after he...

ROSE: Oh Christ, is that why you wanted to look? (*Kate nods yes*) Shit, sorry. You should've said.

KATE: I did – at the top of my voice.

ROSE: I didn't think you meant it.

Enter, at this moment, Christine on the arm of Jenner. There's more than a little of the actress in her 'smiling through-the-tears' approach.

CHRISTINE: I'm not angry. I'm just this side of hysteria but I'm not angry. (*Slight pause*) I didn't kill James. I have to say that in my defence. I did everything I could to keep him alive.

Enter Jennifer, who has been crying. They stand in line as she walks past.

...Happy now?

JENNIFER: Extremely sad.

CHRISTINE: You've killed my husband and wrecked my life...

KATE: Couldn't you have told us how ill he was? So we could say a last goodbye.

JENNIFER: I didn't know. He said he felt fine.

KATE: Not even to let Mum talk to him.

JENNIFER: I'll make sure his child knows what a wonderful man he was.

Jennifer exits

CHRISTINE: Come on Kate. I must pack. (*She walks off with Kate*)

KATE: Yes Mum you pack. We'll leave George and Malcolm to plot in peace...

ROSE: I don't plot Kate. It's not the right word. (*Exit Kate*)

JENNER: This is good. Can't very well accuse you of hating him if you're at his funeral.

ROSE: That's not the reason I'm here.

JENNER: Even stronger. If it's out of respect... even affection. (*Pause*) Pen a letter to the papers now. How sad you are, how much you admired James as a politician and family man, his fine record as our MP. Build your image as a person who can disagree but be reasonable about it, who can heal us, who can move us forward. Before James' team start blaming you for his death.

ROSE: I'll write what I can. The bits I feel are true. I can't start being a hypocrite.

JENNER: Write. Dress the wounds. You need to make an impression and fast. Be seen as a good man. Put yourself in pole position to take over from James.

ROSE: I'll think carefully. Then I'll write.

JENNER: Don't think for too long. We'll have to work like buggary to repair the damage that's been done. We really will have to work like slaves.

END OF SCENE

END OF PLAY